Learn to play
sax

Learn to play
Sax

Ollie Weston

CHARTWELL
BOOKS, INC.

A Quarto Book

Published in 2010 by
Chartwell Books, Inc.
A division of Book Sales, Inc.
276 Fifth Avenue, Suite 206
New York, New York 10001
USA

Copyright 2010 Quarto Inc.

ISBN-13: 978-0-7858-2656-9
ISBN-10: 0-7858-2656-4
QUAR.SAX

Conceived, designed, and produced by
Quarto Publishing plc
The Old Brewery
6 Blundell Street
London N7 9BH

Senior editor: Ruth Patrick
Art editor: Emma Clayton
Designer: Anna Plucinska
Design assistant: Saffron Stocker
Art director: Caroline Guest
Photographer: Simon Pask
Illustrator: Kuo Kang Chen
Picture researcher: Sarah Bell
Proofreader: Sally MacEachern
Indexer: Ann Barrett

Creative director: Moira Clinch
Publisher: Paul Carslake

Color separation in China by
Modern Age Pte Ltd.
Printed in China by Midas Printing
International Pte Ltd.

Contents

Foreword

By picking up this book you've taken your first step toward becoming the saxophone player you've always wanted to be. In writing this book I've tried to give you a thorough introduction to the saxophone—you will learn your way around the instrument from top to bottom at your own pace. You will also learn how to read written music, an invaluable skill that will allow you to play and discover music that you may never have heard before.

The book covers a large range of styles—the saxophone has a huge presence in many different forms of music and I've introduced some of the many styles in the pieces, allowing you to experience the world of music while developing your skills. While not overly theoretical, some important music theory topics are covered too, allowing you to unlock some of the tricks of the trade used by generations of musicians. Good luck and enjoy your saxophone playing!

Ollie Weston

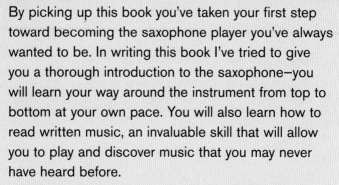

About this book

Lessons

The book begins with 21 lessons covering all you need to know about playing the saxophone, including how to read music, fingering for the notes, and the basics of music theory.

NEW NOTES
A full explanation of how to play each new note is featured, including techniques on how to master any tricky fingering.

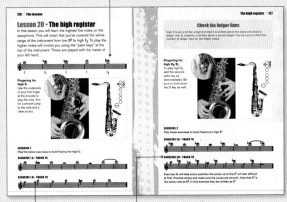

PRACTICE EXERCISES
Practice exercises are featured in each lesson. If a backing track is included on the CD, the track number is given.

BACKING TRACKS ON CD
In the early part of the book the tracks feature the exercise played on the sax. In later pieces, the tracks feature accompaniment with different instruments for you to play along with, followed by the accompaniment and sax, allowing you to check any tricky rhythms.

Fingering charts

A quick-reference fingering guide is featured, consisting of diagrams, charts, and photography, showing all the notes covered in the book.

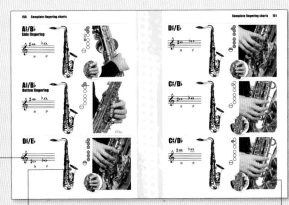

MUSIC
Each note is shown on the stave, helping you to quickly recognize it in its musical context.

FINGERING DIAGRAMS
A fingering diagram for each note is featured, with the red markers showing which keys to press.

PHOTOGRAPHS
Photographs of the right and left hands, showing finger positions and keys.

Scale library

A scale library details the most common scales and modes in each key, as well as twelve-bar blues chord sequences, arpeggios, and chord voicings.

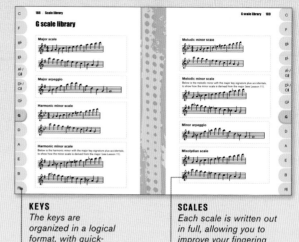

KEYS
The keys are organized in a logical format, with quick-reference tabs at the edge of each page.

SCALES
Each scale is written out in full, allowing you to improve your fingering techniques and fluency on the saxophone.

Practical advice

The practical advice section covers the different types of saxophone, and includes information on accessories, caring for your sax, practice, and joining a band.

SAX RANGES
The upper and lower ranges of each saxophone are given, showing the difference between its concert and written pitch (see page 214).

KEY PLAYERS
Inspirational photographs of key players of each type of sax in action are featured.

Keys on the saxophone

Here is a guide to the keys on the saxophone, along with page references to where the keys are introduced. Some keys are used to play more than one note, in which case they are referred to by a general name.

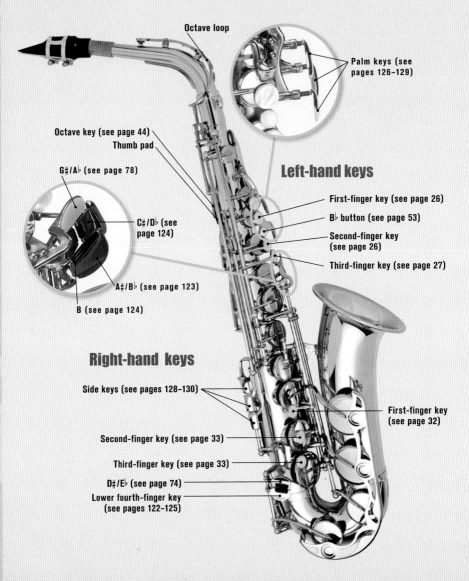

Octave loop

Palm keys (see pages 126–129)

Octave key (see page 44)

Thumb pad

G♯/A♭ (see page 78)

C♯/D♭ (see page 124)

A♯/B♭ (see page 123)

B (see page 124)

Left-hand keys

First-finger key (see page 26)

B♭ button (see page 53)

Second-finger key (see page 26)

Third-finger key (see page 27)

Right-hand keys

Side keys (see pages 128–130)

First-finger key (see page 32)

Second-finger key (see page 33)

Third-finger key (see page 33)

D♯/E♭ (see page 74)

Lower fourth-finger key (see pages 122–125)

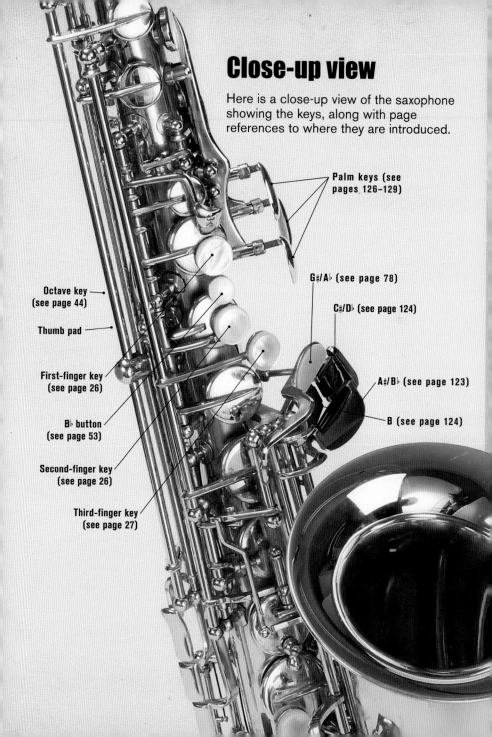

Close-up view

Here is a close-up view of the saxophone showing the keys, along with page references to where they are introduced.

Palm keys (see pages 126–129)

G#/A♭ (see page 78)

C#/D♭ (see page 124)

Octave key (see page 44)

Thumb pad

A#/B♭ (see page 123)

First-finger key (see page 26)

B (see page 124)

B♭ button (see page 53)

Second-finger key (see page 26)

Third-finger key (see page 27)

First-finger key
(see page 32)

Second-finger
key (see page 33)

Third-finger key
(see page 33)

Side keys (see
pages 128–130)

High F♯ key
(see page 130)

D♯/E♭
(see page 74)

Lower fourth-finger key
(see pages 122–125)

History of the saxophone

This chapter will introduce you to Antoine-Joseph "Adolphe" Sax, the inventor of the saxophone, and some of the instruments that preceded the saxophone and influenced its design.

Adolphe Sax and the bass clarinet

Adolphe Sax was born in 1814 in the town of Dinant in Belgium. Sax's father Charles Joseph Sax was an instrument designer and manufacturer himself and the young Adolphe was fascinated and inspired by the work he saw going on in his father's workshop. By the age of six the young Adolphe had a well-developed sense of the mechanics of most wind and brass instruments and was fully able to assist his father in the design and manufacturing of his instruments. Adolphe was also an accomplished performer, attending the Brussels Conservatory of Music and excelling on the flute and clarinet.

In 1830, while still a teenager, Adolphe Sax sent two flutes and a clarinet of his making to the Brussels Industrial Exhibition. The instruments were well received and considered to be fine examples of top-quality instrument craftsmanship. Sax's big break came when he modified the bass clarinet–the previously cumbersome and difficult clarinet was hugely improved by Sax who, among other things, added keys to cover the holes rather than having open holes that were covered by the fingers. The new instrument had a more even sound and was able to project more clearly than its predecessor, making it a welcome addition to the woodwind section of the orchestra.

Bass clarinet
Making improvements to the bass clarinet established Sax's reputation as a craftsman and instrument designer.

Adolphe Sax
A portrait of Adolphe Sax, dated *c.*1860.

Sax unveiled his new instrument at an orchestral event in Brussels much to the dismay of the existing bass clarinettist who was unimpressed with Sax's modifications. The pugnacious Sax challenged the man to a kind of musical duel of bass clarinet playing—Sax's excellent musicianship coupled with his much-improved instrument were too good for the existing bass clarinettist and Sax's new instrument was hailed a success. This was not to be the first confrontation in Sax's life—he was often met with resistance by the musical establishment and by jealous musicians.

The invention of the saxophone

In 1841, Adolphe Sax left Belgium for
Paris. He had begun to forge a reputation
as a musician and instrument designer
par excellence and was keen to live in
the thriving cultural center of Paris. It
was during this time that Sax's instrument
inventing became more prolific and he
made early prototypes of the saxophone.
His main aim was to combine the power
and sound quality of a brass instrument,
such as the trumpet or trombone, with the
agility and flexibility of a woodwind instrument
like the flute or clarinet. This had been attempted
before with instruments called the "serpent"
and the "ophicleide"–although used by some
of the leading composers of the day including
Berlioz and Wagner, the ophicleide and the
serpent haven't really stood the test of time and
mostly appear as novelty museum pieces.

Ophicleide
An early attempt to combine
the keywork of a wind
instrument with a brass
instrument's mouthpiece.

After much trial and error
in the early 1840s, Sax
found a combination he
was happy with and in 1846
filed a patent for his new
instrument: the saxophone.
The first example of the
saxophone is believed to
have been a bigger version
of the instrument similar to
today's baritone saxophone,
rather than the predominant
alto and tenor.

XXVI   *Serpentone*

Serpent
The long tube required to produce the
deeper sound was curved like a snake.

The saxophone and the orchestra

The instrument was received particularly well by the maverick French composer Hector Berlioz who wrote a glowing review of both Sax and his new instrument. Berlioz, like Sax, was a controversial figure attracting plaudits for his groundbreaking work but also ruffling the feathers of the musical establishment with his unorthodox techniques.

Despite Berlioz's endorsement, the saxophone has never become a mainstream orchestral instrument—the huge amount of repertoire composed before the saxophone's invention had made a firm blueprint for the instrumentation of the symphony orchestra. The instrument does feature in some works (Ravel's "Bolero" and Mussorgsky's "Pictures At An Exhibition" are two famous examples), however the saxophone has never found its full-time home in the orchestra.

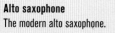

Alto saxophone
The modern alto saxophone.

The saxophone in military bands

Adolphe Sax's commercial breakthrough came when he persuaded the French War Minister to adopt his instrument in the military bands. The previously used ophicleide and bassoon couldn't compete in the open air with the brass instruments and the louder woodwind instruments, so the saxophone seemed a perfect choice to fill the gap. After initial reservations (the French were unimpressed with a Belgian inventor telling them how to run their military!) the instrument found its place. The use of the saxophone in military bands was so popular that it began to be used outside of France. Military bands all over Europe started to add the bold, brassy new instrument to their ranks. This adoption

of the saxophone by the military is arguably the most important thing to have happened to the instrument in its youth because this led to it being played all over the world and its eventual use in jazz and other contemporary idioms. It is hard to imagine this happening had Adolphe Sax not lobbied the French minister.

By the time of his death in 1894, Adolphe Sax was presiding over a new saxophone class at the Paris Conservatory of Music, and although still having to fight off his jealous rivals and their claims of the illegitimacy of his invention, Sax had successfully created an instrument that would change music forever.

Military band
Ceremonial parade on Kiev main street, Ukraine.

Saxophone in band
Musicians at the Festival of Military Bands, St. Petersburg, Russia.

1 The Lessons

The 21 lessons that follow cover the basics of the saxophone from assembly and basic fingerings to the high and low extremes of the range and all the notes in between. The lessons also introduce you to written music and notation, allowing you to develop your theoretical skills simultaneously.

Lesson 1 • Assembly and producing your first sound

Opening the saxophone case for the first time can be a bewildering experience. You will recognize the main body of the instrument, but notice also that the saxophone has a few sections that you need to put together each time you play. Initially this might take you a few minutes but as you do it more often it will become easy.

1. MOUTHPIECE
As the name suggests, the mouthpiece is the part of the saxophone that goes in your mouth. The reed sits on the flat section with the tip of the reed reaching almost to the tip of the mouthpiece—you should be able to see a pencil line's worth of the mouthpiece behind the reed (see above).

Saxophone reeds

The reed is the part of the saxophone that actually produces the sound. The vibrations caused by blowing the reed resonate through the instrument and produce the distinctive saxophone sound. Reeds do crack and split and so need replacing—how often depends on how much you play but every few weeks is a good rule of thumb. The tip is also quite fragile so handle with care. You will need to moisten the reed with saliva before you play; a dry reed doesn't vibrate well and won't sound too good.

The reed comes in a protective plastic case. Always remove the reed from the mouthpiece and slide it back into the cover when you've finished, since this will protect it when it's not in use.

2. THE CROOK
The next step is to attach the mouthpiece to the crook and the crook to the saxophone. The crook is the curved section at the top of the instrument. The end is lined with cork to allow you to attach the mouthpiece easily—the amount you push the mouthpiece on determines the tuning (push it all the way on and the note will be higher, pull it back and the note will be lower.) Aim to cover about half of the cork with the mouthpiece. If you are finding it difficult to slide the mouthpiece on, you can lubricate the cork with the cork grease provided with your saxophone. This usually comes in a small tube similar to a lipstick and will moisten the cork on the crook.

3. THE LIGATURE

The ligature is used to hold the reed in place on the mouthpiece. The screws need to be on the same side as the reed and be tightened sufficiently to hold the reed in place, but not over tightly, since this will hamper the reed's vibration and affect the sound quality.

4. MAIN BODY

Finally, insert the crook into the main body of the saxophone to complete assembly, loosening the screw on the top of the body of the saxophone first. This should be tightened enough to stop the crook sliding around when you are playing, but try not to overtighten it.

Travel and storage

The saxophone is disassembled to make transportation easier. You can use either a hard case or a soft case (see Practical advice, page 228).

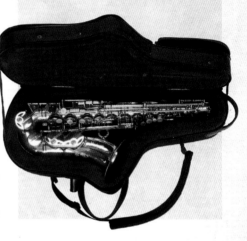

5. THE SLING

To keep the saxophone safe while you are playing as well as to provide support for your arms, the saxophone has a sling that goes around your neck. Attach the clip to the ring halfway up the back of the instrument. Then adjust the height so that the mouthpiece is level with your mouth.

TOP TUNE–JAZZ
Lester Young–"Lady Be Good"
This 1936 recording of the Gershwin classic captures Lester Young at his peak.

Producing your first sound

To make your first sound on the saxophone, use just the mouthpiece and crook. This will allow you to get used to blowing and breathing without the extra distraction of holding the instrument.

Embouchure

The embouchure is the position your mouth needs to be in to make a good sound. Your front teeth should rest on the top of the mouthpiece (the side without the reed) and the reed should rest on your bottom lip, the lip curling slightly over your bottom teeth to act as a cushion. Aim to put about half an inch of the mouthpiece into your mouth.

All the air pressure involved in playing the saxophone should be produced by your diaphragm (the muscles in your stomach around the lungs) rather than your face muscles. If you are screwing up your face you are trying too hard! The golden rule is that you should never puff out your cheeks.

Now blow through the mouthpiece and try to push the air up from your stomach into the mouthpiece—aim for a steady, even note. Hold the note for as long as possible (at least 10 seconds) without any wobbles or surges in volume. This will help you control your breathing and produce an even, rich sound.

Incorrect embouchure
Puffed-out cheeks will provide a weak airstream and uncontrollable sound.

Correct embouchure
Direct the air from your stomach muscles into the mouthpiece and aim for a narrow stream of air.

Articulation

As in speech, saxophone playing uses the tongue to articulate notes. You should use your tongue to start the notes rather than just starting to blow.

Think of three words beginning with the letter "T" and repeat them round and round—"toast, tea, tiger," "toast, tea, tiger." Note that it is the phonetic sound of the "T" that is important. As you say the words, notice how the tongue flicks the ridge behind your two front teeth.

Now try the same thing but with the saxophone mouthpiece and crook in your mouth. Place your tongue on the tip of the reed and then release it with a strong "T" sound. The air from your diaphragm should be ready behind the tongue as you release.

Using the tongue to articulate the start of the note gives your notes a clear and definite beginning. Spend some time practicing starting notes with clear tonguing and then holding them steadily as before. Then start to add different rhythms and try to tongue a note every second.

Your final exercise before playing the whole instrument is to pick out some

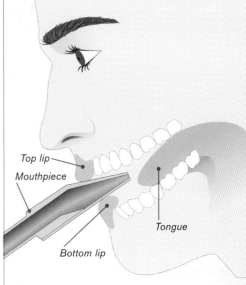

Top lip
Mouthpiece
Tongue
Bottom lip

Clear tonguing
Use your tongue to cover the reed and block the airflow into the mouthpiece.

rhythms of your own. Start with some favorite songs and try to follow the rhythm of the tune (we will add the notes later.) If you're stuck for ideas, think of your favorite band, Christmas carol, or TV or film soundtrack.

Buying reeds

Reeds are a fragile and disposable part of the saxophone, so it's important to keep a supply of spares. They are usually sold in boxes of 10, so keep the box in your case and you won't be caught short. Reeds come in different thicknesses from 1 (thinnest) to 5 (thickest) with half sizes in between. The thicker the reed the harder it is to blow. As a beginner you should have a fairly soft reed—go for a box of 1 ½ or 2 strength to start with. Once a reed is cracked or split, it's time to throw it away and start using the next one.

There are many different reed manufacturers—Rico and Vandoren are the most common. The choice is very subjective and most saxophonists have a favorite brand arrived at through trial and error.

Lesson 2 •
Holding the saxophone and first notes

In Lesson 1 you learned how to produce your first sounds on the saxophone using just the mouthpiece and the crook. Hopefully you are now comfortable with the principles of breathing, blowing, and sound production and are making a steady, even sound with the mouthpiece and crook. Remember to use your tongue to articulate the notes (see page 23).

ATTACHING THE CROOK
The first step is to put the crook and mouthpiece into the top of the saxophone. Loosen the screw on the top of the saxophone to allow the crook in and then tighten to hold it in place.

HOLDING THE SAXOPHONE
Because the saxophone is quite heavy you should use the sling to support the instrument as you are playing. Put the sling around your neck and attach it to the instrument with the hook on the back of the saxophone. Adjust the height so that the mouthpiece is at the same level as your mouth. Try to stand up straight—you shouldn't be leaning forward or backward to reach the mouthpiece.

Fingering charts

The fingerings for different notes are usually represented on a chart. This is usually in the form of a diagram of the saxophone with certain keys colored in to show that they are to be pressed down or "closed" (see overleaf).

The left hand

Your left hand is always higher up the instrument than your right. Put your left thumb on the black pad on the back of the saxophone and curl the rest of your hand around so that your fingers are facing away from you at the front.

Your left hand fingers should then find three keys that correspond with your first, second, and third fingers. Ignore the smaller key in between your first and second fingers, you will use this later.

The right hand

Your right hand thumb should sit under the hook on the back of the saxophone just below the sling attachment.

Your right hand curves around the instrument so that your fingers are facing forward. You won't be using your right hand to produce any notes in this lesson but get used to the position of your right thumb because it will help you to balance the instrument.

First notes: B, A, G, and C

Spend a little time getting used to playing these four notes. You can jump from low to high or vice versa if you wish—just try to keep an even sound and smooth movement. Once you are comfortable with this you can move onto Lesson 3 where you will see these notes written as music and then start to play some proper tunes.

Fingering for B

With your left thumb still on the black pad at the back, put your first finger down—this note is a B.

Notice how the finger is curved rather than flat, which allows your finger to move more smoothly and will result in a quicker technique.

Fingering for A

If you add your second finger while playing a B, you will get an A—this is lower than B. Remember that you are adding your second finger and your first finger stays down.

TOP TUNE–JAZZ CHARLIE PARKER "NIGHT IN TUNISIA"
Recorded during the legendary Dial Sessions in the 1940s, this is bebop at its best. Listen out for the famous alto saxophone break.

Fingering for G
If you add your third finger, you will produce the note G, lower than A.

Fingering for C
The next note we will learn is C. This is one step higher than B and is played by using just your second finger. Try to play each note for four seconds—you are aiming for an even sound, and there should be no wobbles in the notes. Move smoothly between the notes without any unwanted "extra" notes appearing by accident! Remember to keep your fingers curved and relaxed.

Lesson 3 • Notation and rhythm

In this lesson you will see music written down for the first time and see how to relate the written notes to the notes you've learned in Lesson 2.

Reading music

Reading music is an essential skill for you to develop. Although some great musicians have survived purely on playing "by ear" and using their creativity and intuition, it is important to know how to read music from a written page. This allows you to play unfamiliar music and broaden your repertoire, and also allows you to play in groups when more often than not the music will be played from written scores.

The system of writing music evolved in European classical music and has remained essentially unchanged for hundreds of years.

THE STAVE
The set of five horizontal lines running across the page is called a "stave." An empty stave is a musical blank canvas onto which you write the notes.

TREBLE CLEF
The ornate symbol to the left of the stave is called a "treble clef." This tells us that we are in the higher end of the sound world—some instruments make a higher sound than others and so there are different clefs for different instruments. Lower-sounding instruments—cello, double bass, trombone etc.—are written on a bass clef. Instruments such as the piano have a huge range covering both the treble and bass clefs, so pianists need to be able to read both treble and bass clef. The saxophone is written in treble clef—look for the symbol at the left side of the music.

BAR LINES
The horizontal lines going through the stave are called "bar lines." These divide the music up into small chunks called "bars." Each bar is a set length in time measured in beats—four beats per bar is the most common although you can have bars of different lengths, as we will discover later.

Notes on the stave

You'll notice that there are two letter Es and letter Fs—this is because music uses only seven different notes: A, B, C, D, E, F, and G. This set of seven notes then repeat but higher or lower. A set of eight notes is called an "octave," and a saxophone has a range of about two and a half octaves in total. Soon you will recognize the notes quickly from the stave—just remember that the bottom line is an E and count up the lines and spaces alphabetically. Look back to Lesson 2 and the four notes you learned—G, A, B, and C.

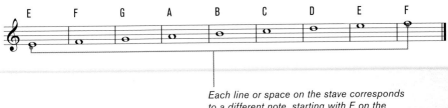

Each line or space on the stave corresponds to a different note, starting with E on the bottom line to F on the top line. The notes ascend by step through the alphabet.

Notes G, A, B, and C

Here are G, A, B, and C written on the stave. Playing these four notes should now be comfortable for you—now play them while reading them from the stave. Try to get used to relating the written notes to the position of your fingers. For now you'll have the names of the notes written above the stave to help you, but you won't always have that luxury.

Rhythm

Any written note will give you two pieces of information—the pitch of the note and the length. Initially we will use three different lengths of note: 4 beats, 2 beats, and 1 beat.

Whole-note, half-note, and quarter-note

In the United States and in more contemporary music—rock and jazz in particular—the notes are often referred to by their relative lengths. A "whole-note" has four beats, a "half-note" has two beats, and a "quarter-note" has one beat. This makes the relationship between the notes easier to understand. In Europe, musical notation has Italian names—the different notes are referred to as "semibreve" (four beats long) "minim" (two beats long), and "crotchet" (one beat long.)

Note	American Name	European Name	Value
𝅝	Whole-note	Semibreve	4 beats
𝅗𝅥	Half-note	Minim	2 beats
𝅘𝅥	Quarter-note	Crotchet	1 beat

EXERCISE 1 · TRACK 1

Play through Exercise 4, make sure you are keeping a pulse. Rhythm is important, since a half-note is only a half-note if it's half a whole-note. Use a clock and count each second as one beat. Each of these three bars is the same length and uses the three different note lengths to make a complete four-beat bar.

Whole-note/Semibreve   Half-note/Minim   Quarter-note/Crotchet

EXERCISES 2, 3, AND 4

See if you can play these three tunes that mix up the different note lengths with the four notes you've learned—remember to keep a strong pulse, but the speed of each beat is up to you. Try each piece at different speeds and practice counting whole-notes, half-notes, and quarter-notes.

EXERCISE 2 · TRACK 2

> **TOP TUNE–CLASSICAL/ CONTEMPORARY**
> **Jan Garbarek "Officium"**
> Garbarek's unique musical vision led him to pair his haunting tenor and soprano saxophone playing with a male voice Gregorian ensemble–the result was a runaway success appealing to fans of both jazz and classical music.

EXERCISE 3 · TRACK 3

EXERCISE 4 · TRACK 4

Lesson 4 •
Using the right hand

You should now be comfortable playing G, A, B, and C and using these to play the practice tunes (see page 31). You are hopefully now comfortable reading these notes from the stave and playing whole-notes, half-notes, and quarter-notes. In this lesson you will start to use your right hand and add three more notes to your repertoire: F, E, and D. These notes are lower than those previously learned.

Right hand thumb
Your right thumb provides balance and supports the weight of the saxophone by sitting under the hook at the back of the instrument.

Fingering for F
To play an F you need to keep your left hand as if it's playing a G (this is the same for all the low notes), then add the first finger of your right hand onto the highest of the three keys under your right hand. Try not to move your finger too far—always rest it on the key when not in use rather than coming from a great height.

Fingering for E

To play an E,
add your second
finger to the
F fingering. To
move from E to F
you only need to move
one finger—get used to
leaving your left hand
with three fingers over
the keys.

Fingering for D

Add your third
finger to the E
fingering to play
a low D. You have
now closed more
of the saxophone and
made a longer tube,
resulting in a lower
note. Remember to
keep your fingers nicely
curved and rest them
lightly on the keys when
not in use.

Playing the low notes

To get used to the sound and feel of the low notes try to play each as a long
note. As in Lesson 1, try to hold each note for as long as possible (aim for
10 seconds plus). Remember the notes should be even and wobble-free!
Resist the temptation to tense up your embouchure—keep relaxed and the
notes will sound clear, rich, and sonorous. When you are comfortable
playing each of the low notes, try some of the following exercises. Make sure
that you count the half-notes and quarter-notes accurately.

EXERCISE 1 · TRACK 5

EXERCISE 2 · TRACK 6

EXERCISE 3 · TRACK 7

Intervals

The distance between two notes is called an interval and is measured numerically from the bottom note to the top note—G to A is an interval of a second, G to B is an interval of a third, and so on. When working through the practice tunes later in the book, ask yourself how they start and with which interval—see the play list below for some tunes for you to start with.

EXERCISE 4

The widest available intervals between the seven notes you have learned is a seventh—from the low D to the C. Practice moving between the two notes.

EXERCISE 5 • TRACK 8

You can now also make the interval of a fifth, which is a very common interval in music. Here are three examples of intervals of a fifth. The space between the lower and the higher note is a fifth.

Play list

To get you playing and also thinking about music here are some famous melodies to play. Only the name of the tune and the first couple of notes are given—see if you can work out the rest. This technique is called "playing by ear"— ask yourself if the next note is higher or lower than the one you are playing and then try to find it by trial and error.

"Amazing Grace" This gospel classic starts on a low D and moves to a G—this is an interval of a fourth.

"In the Jungle" From Disney's *The Lion King* starts on a G and moves up a second to A and then another second from A to B.

If you can work out these melodies quickly you are doing well—it can take time to develop your musical ear.

Lesson 5 • Time signatures and rests

Lesson 3 introduced the concepts of bars and bar lines. You will remember that bars can be of different lengths. At the start of the piece of music there is a sign called a "time signature." In this lesson we will explore time signatures and their different meanings as well as some practical uses for different time signatures.

Time signatures

The blank stave below has four empty bars with a time signature next to the treble clef. The two fours on top of each other make the time signature and tell us that we are in "four four" time.

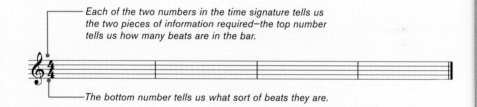

Each of the two numbers in the time signature tells us the two pieces of information required—the top number tells us how many beats are in the bar.

The bottom number tells us what sort of beats they are.

Whole-notes, half-notes, and quarter-notes in a time signature

In Lesson 3, the main note lengths were introduced: whole-notes, half-notes, and quarter-notes. These terms help you to easily understand the bottom number within a time signature. If you think of a quarter-note as a fraction, the bottom number would be a 4—one quarter is written as 1/4. Therefore when you see a four at the bottom of a time signature you know that the units of that bar are quarter-notes. The top 4 tells us that there are four of those units per bar. So 4/4 means four quarter-note beats per bar.

EXERCISE 1 • TRACK 9
Here are four bars of 4/4 time with various rhythms—note that the contents of each bar add up to four quarter-notes.

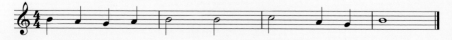

EXERCISE 2 • TRACK 10

If you change the bottom number to a 2, you change the unit of time
to half-notes. So 2/2 means that there are two half-notes per bar.

You'll notice that 4/4 and 2/2 are very similar and both contain the same
combinations of notes required to make a complete bar. 2/2 is usually
used at very fast tempos when it would be hard to count 4 beats per bar.

EXERCISE 3 • TRACK 11

Here are some other time signatures—try to work out what they mean
and count up the beats in each to see that they contain the correct
number of beats. Always look at the bottom number because that will
tell you the unit that you are dealing with for any time signature: 1/2,
1/4, 1/1 etc.

In each of the above examples make sure that you understand what
each of the two numbers in the time signature means and that you are
comfortable adding up the beats of the bar to make the total. In the
above examples, 3/4 means there are three quarter (quarter-note) beats
per bar. 3/2 means there are three half (half-note) beats per bar, and
2/4 means there are two quarter (quarter-note) beats per bar.

Rests

Every note length has an equivalent rest that indicates a silence for a certain amount of time. Music relies on silence for effect and so it's important that you are familiar with rest symbols.

Note	American Name	European Name	Value
▬	Whole-note rest	Semibreve rest	4 beats
▬	Half-note rest	Minim rest	2 beats
𝄽	Quarter-note rest	Crotchet rest	1 beat

TOP TUNE–FILM/TV
Plas Johnson–The Pink Panther theme with Henry Mancini
Henry Mancini's legendary theme has possibly inspired more people to take up the saxophone than anything else. Plas Johnson's husky tenor defined the cool sound of the Pink Panther films.

EXERCISE 4 • TRACK 12

Here is a bar of quarter-notes followed by a bar of quarter-note rests (note that this example is in 4/4 time). Each of the four symbols in the second bar indicates a quarter-note rest.

EXERCISE 5 · TRACK 13

Now clap or play the next example. Set up a pulse with your foot
and get used to letting a beat pass with no note—you should only
be playing or clapping on beats 1 and 3 of the two bars. Loop
these two bars until you are comfortable doing this.

EXERCISE 6 · TRACK 14

In the next example the rests and quarter-notes are swapped so
that the notes are on the second and fourth beats of each bar.

EXERCISE 7 · TRACK 15

Half-note rests work in exactly the same way—here is a half-note
followed by a half-note rest.

EXERCISE 8 · TRACK 16

Here they are the other way around.

EXERCISE 9 · TRACK 17

A whole-note rest looks very similar to a half-note rest, but it hangs
from the second from top line of the stave rather than the half-note
rest, which sits on top of the middle line.

Play or clap Exercises 5–9 until you are comfortable counting notes and
rests. The important thing to remember is that the pulse continues
throughout the rests; keep a tap going with your foot and make sure that
you feel the rests as they are passing. Work out on which beat of the bar
there are notes and come in confidently after the rests.

Coleman Hawkins
November 21, 1904–May 19, 1969

PLAYER PROFILE

Hawkins is arguably the father of the tenor saxophone. Before
him, the instrument wasn't used much outside military bands
and was considered a rather coarse and inflexible instrument.
In Coleman Hawkins' hands the tenor saxophone became a
rich, sonorous instrument that has influenced generations of
players and come to typify the sound of jazz.

Hawkins was born in Missouri but arrived in New York in the
early 1920s where he made his name as a featured soloist in
Fletcher Henderson's Orchestra—the band briefly boasted
Louis Armstrong as a member and Hawkins' style was hugely
influenced by Armstrong.

Hawkins left the United States in the 1930s and toured
Europe before returning to the States and recording his most
famous piece—a breathtaking version of the classic standard
"Body and Soul."

Coleman Hawkins' sound and phrasing as well as his melodic and harmonic invention had
a profound effect on the next generation of saxophone players—most notably bebop legend
Sonny Rollins, who recorded an album with his idol in 1963 entitled *Sonny Meets Hawk*.

Key recordings: "Body and Soul," 1939; *Coleman Hawkins Encounters Ben Webster*, 1957;
Sonny Meets Hawk, 1963.

Dotted notes

You may have noticed that there hasn't yet been a symbol for a three-beat note or rest? There isn't a new symbol for a three-beat note, but instead a dot placed by a half-note.

A dot next to a note or rest indicates that it is increased in length by half of its own value. So in the case of a half-note, you simply halve the note and add that half onto the original: half of 2 is 1, and added to 2 this makes 3. Think of a store sale that advertises 50 percent extra free...

A dotted half-note is the most common of the dotted notes, but it's possible to have dotted quarter-notes too as we will discover later in the book.

EXERCISE 10 • TRACK 18
Practice playing or clapping Exercise 10 until you are comfortable with a three-beat note and rest.

Musical uses of different time signatures

Apart from dividing written music up into smaller, readable chunks, different time signatures have different implications within music. The convention is to stress the first beat of the bar and so create a stronger beat and a rhythmic pattern. Different types of music rely on these rhythmic patterns for their effect. Two good examples are the march and the waltz.

March music

Marches are a great example of music that takes its rhythmic emphasis from the time signature. March music grew from military music and is usually in 2/4 time. The stress on beat one of each bar accompanies the footsteps of marching soldiers.

March music usually has a ceremonial or military air to it. Good examples are Sir Edward Elgar's "Pomp and Circumstance March No. 1" or the "Imperial March" (Darth Vadar's theme) from the *The Empire Strikes Back*.

PRACTICE TUNE "QUICK MARCH" • TRACK 19
Play through "Quick March" with the backing track and feel the effect of the 2/4 time signature. Stress the first beat of the bar for a grand ceremonial feel to the tune.

Waltz music

In the same way that marches are easily identified by their time signatures, waltzes are another style of music that have a strong rhythmic feel. The waltz is a traditional European dance and is always in 3 time, again with the first beat of each bar emphasized.

Johann Strauss was a famous composer of waltz music, so much so that he was known as the "Waltz King." His "Blue Danube" is one of his most famous pieces and illustrates the waltz feel perfectly. "My Favorite Things" from Rogers and Hammerstein's *The Sound of Music* is another classic waltz.

EXERCISE 11 · TRACK 20

Exercise 11 has four bars of waltz time written out—practice clapping or playing these bars and stressing the first beat of each bar.

PRACTICE TUNE "WALTZ FOR THREE" · TRACK 21

Now play through "Waltz for Three" with the backing track. Give the first beat of each bar an accent, which will help you to create an authentic waltz feel. Watch out for the rests too...

Lesson 6 • Crossing the break

In this lesson you are going to double your repertoire of notes by learning how to use one more key—the octave key.

The octave key

If you look above your left thumb, you will see a key that is shaped around the black pad. This is called the "octave key" and as the name suggests, alters notes by an octave (eight notes).

Your left thumb rests on the black pad and operates the octave key. Opening and closing the octave key allows you to move from the low register (the bottom of the saxophone range) to the middle and high registers in one motion.

In Lesson 3, you learned how there are only seven different note names—A, B, C, D, E, F, and G—before they start to repeat. There are, for example, two different Es on the stave. Both of these notes are Es; however, the second one is eight notes or an "octave" higher. The good news is that to play both notes on the saxophone doesn't need any other fingering than the octave key.

EXERCISE 1

Play a low E and while holding it, add the octave key with your thumb. Don't move your whole thumb to play the note—you should operate the octave key simply by bending the joint of your thumb. The base of your thumb should never leave the black pad.

E   E

Left thumb technique
Keep your thumb in contact with the pad at all times—to operate the key, just flex your thumb joint.

The low E should jump smoothly up to the higher note. It can be hard to control but aim for a smooth movement to the higher note without any surges or wobbles.

EXERCISE 2

All the notes you've already learned can now be played an octave higher simply by adding the octave key. Look back to Lessons 2 and 4 for a reminder of the fingerings—remember that you only have to press the octave key to play the higher notes. Note that high A, B, and C are above the basic stave—think of the "ledger lines" running through the notes as a continuation of the stave.

D   E   F   G   A   B   C

EXERCISE 3 · TRACK 22

Practice the following exercise to get used to jumping up an octave—try to keep an even sound with a good transition between the low and high notes.

D   D   E   E   F   F   G   G   A   A   B   B   C   C

Slurs and tongued notes

So far we have concentrated on tonguing all the
notes. As in speech, articulation is very important for
saxophone playing because it makes your playing crisp
and clear. However sometimes the music requires a
smoother approach with the notes joined together
and played without the tongue. This is called a "slur."
Try playing two notes (any two will do) next to each
other without tonguing them—the only thing that should
move is your finger to change the note; your mouth
position should remain the same and your tongue
shouldn't move. A slur on a piece of music is indicated
by a curved line joining the two notes.

EXERCISE 4 • TRACK 23
Practice slurring between the notes below until you are
comfortable and moving smoothly between them—remember
that you still need to tongue the first note of any slurred group
of notes.

Then practice slurring between different pairs of the notes in your
repertoire. The hardest move is from C to D when you have to put
down lots of fingers at once. Make sure all of your fingers touch
the keys simultaneously.

TOP TUNE–POP/FUNK/SOUL
Branford Marsalis "Little Wing" with Sting
From Sting's 1987 album *Nothing Like the
Sun*, Marsalis' pristine soprano saxophone
sound adds a touch of class to this Jimi
Hendrix tune.

PRACTICE TUNE "JOIN THE DOTS" • TRACK 24

This piece combines the higher register you've learned in this chapter with slurs. "Join the Dots" is a jazz-style piece and should sound relaxed and effortless. Aim for a rich sound on the higher notes and pay attention to the slurs.

Lester Young
August 27, 1909–March 15, 1959

Lester Young was an early pioneer of the tenor saxophone. He enjoyed a healthy rivalry with Coleman Hawkins (see page 40) as the two vied for the position of the top tenor saxophone man of the 1930s, yet the two were very different players. As opposed to Hawkins' rich and robust tone, Lester Young was light and airy, lending a cool elegance and grace to the previously unfashionable tenor saxophone. Lester Young continued the cool, playful side of his playing into his personality—he often spoke in his own type of slang that the uninitiated found impossible to understand. This coupled with his sharp dress sense and his habit of playing the saxophone nonchalantly at a sideways angle made him a colorful character and one of jazz's real eccentrics. Nicknamed the "President of the Saxophone" by singer Billie Holiday, the name "Pres" stuck with him for most of his career.

Lester Young came to prominence in the great Count Basie's Orchestra of the 1930s—luckily, many of the recordings have survived and are a fantastic introduction to Lester Young's playing.

Key recordings: *Count Basie: Lester Young with The Oscar Peterson Trio (Vol. 1 and 2)*, 1954; *The Complete Decca Recordings*, 1992.

Dynamics

The saxophone is capable of a wide range of volumes from pin-drop quiet to loud and brassy. Once you start to control the volume of the saxophone you will open up a wider range of colors and expression to your playing.

As with the European note lengths, the terms used to describe the volume of the saxophone are in Italian. The main terms are:

Marker	Term	Translation
pp	"pianissimo"	very quiet
p	"piano"	quiet
mp	"mezzo piano"	medium quiet
mf	"mezzo forte"	medium loud
f	"forte"	loud
ff	"fortissimo"	very loud

These terms are subjective, but on a scale of 1 to 10, 1 would be "pp" and 10 would be "ff."

Now play "Join the Dots" (see page 47) again at different volumes. The dynamic of a piece is marked underneath the stave. The piece is marked as "mf" (medium loud) so in the middle of your range (6 or 7 out of 10 perhaps) but experiment with different dynamics and see the effect it has. Always check a piece for the dynamics—you don't want to be the one in the band blasting it out when everyone else is pp!

Crescendo and decrescendo

Crescendo and *decrescendo* are used to mark a gradual change of dynamic. On a single note or over a period of a few bars you can indicate a change of volume from quiet to loud ("*crescendo*") or from loud to quiet ("*decrescendo*"). These changes are indicated by a V-shaped symbol positioned under the music—the wide end signals loud and the point signals quiet, so always check which way they are going.

EXERCISE 5 • TRACK 25

The "V" underneath the first C shows that the note gets louder. The second "V" (pointing in the other direction) shows that the note is to get quieter.

Practice crescendos and decrescendos on many different notes until you are comfortable changing the volume of a note in either direction. As always make sure your notes are steady and don't wobble as you increase/decrease the volume.

PRACTICE TUNE "JOIN THE DOTS" • TRACK 24

Here is another version of "Join the Dots," this time with lots of dynamic markings. Try to follow these as well as the notes and see how these details enhance your performance of the tune.

The obvious dynamics of this piece have been followed—quite simply that higher is louder. As the musical line goes up and down the dynamics follow. This is often how music feels that it should go and is a good default for pieces with no dynamic markings.

Lesson 7 • Sharps and flats

So far we have only dealt with seven note names (in two octaves, so technically fourteen notes.) In this lesson you'll be introduced to "sharps" and "flats," collectively known as "accidentals." An accidental can raise or lower a note halfway between it and the next note.

TOP TUNE–JAZZ
Gerry Mulligan
"Walkin' Shoes"
A composition written for the Mulligan/Chet Baker Quartet of the 1950s, this tune showcases Mulligan's sensitive and agile playing of the baritone saxophone.

Introducing sharps

So far you will have assumed that the next available note up from F is G. However there is a note halfway between the two—F sharp or F♯. The easiest way to think of these gaps is to think of them as steps—F to G is a whole step or "tone" whereas F to F♯ is a half step or "semitone." F♯ is higher than an F but not as high as a G.

Fingering for F♯
To play F♯ put your left hand down as if for a G, then add the second finger of your right hand. To play F♯ an octave higher, add the octave key to this fingering.

EXERCISE 1

Practice moving smoothly between F and F♯. If there is an overlap
between the notes you might end up playing an E as well.

EXERCISE 2

Here are few different rhythms to get you used to playing F and
F♯—the half step between F and F♯ sounds a bit like the theme
tune to *Jaws*!

EXERCISE 3 · TRACK 26

Exercise 3 sums up the use of F♯ explained in this lesson. Make
sure you are moving smoothly between F, F♯, and G.

It's important to be sure when you are playing an F or an F♯. To
neutralize a sharp sign you must use a "natural" sign. The below
shows exactly the same music as the above, but the sign by each
of the non-sharpened Fs (F naturals) shows that regular F should
be played.

Introducing flats

In the same way that a sharp is a half step higher than the note indicated, a flat is a half step lower. The sign for a flat looks a little like a lower case b. This note is lower than B but not as low as A.

B♭ can be fingered in different ways on the saxophone—the most common is called the side B♭ fingering (see below). There is an alternate fingering using the B♭ button (see opposite). Both of the fingerings are necessary and you will soon get a feel for which is easier in certain situations, depending on what notes are following.

Side B♭ fingering

With your left hand, finger an A, add the bottom of the three side keys by your right hand. Use the inside of your first finger by the knuckle. Keep your right hand fingers as close to the main three keys as possible. To play B♭ an octave higher, add the octave key to this fingering.

Button B♭ fingering

Between the B and A keys under your left hand there is a smaller key—this is the B♭ "button." You might be tempted to use your second finger to press this key—this means that the second finger is then unavailable to play A if it needs to. Instead use your first finger to press down both the B and B♭ button keys.

EXERCISE 4

Here are two exercises to get you moving between A, B♭, and B natural.

A   B♭   A   B♭   A   B♭   A   B♭

EXERCISE 5 · TRACK 27

Note that the natural sign means that the unflattened note should be played in the same way as for a sharp.

Sharp or flat, or both?

Because a sharp or flat is exactly a semitone (half step) higher or lower than the note in question, it has two different names. The B♭ is a semitone lower than a B, but it is also a semitone higher than an A and so could just as easily be called an A♯. By the same token, the F♯ in Exercises 1, 2, and 3 could also be called a G♭, because it is lower than a G but higher than an F.

The only exceptions to this rule are the gap between E and F and B and C. These are already intervals of a semitone, so E♯ would actually just be an F in the same way the F♭ would be an E. Similarly C♭ is the same as B and B♯ is the same as C. The reason for this slightly asymmetrical division of the octave will become apparent in Lesson 8.

Other sharps and flats will be introduced as we go on but B♭ and F♯ are the most common.

PRACTICE TUNE "FLATLINE" • TRACK 28
Play this tune along with the backing track and get used to playing the B♭s instead of B naturals.

An accidental affects all of the same notes to which the accidental is applied later in the bar.

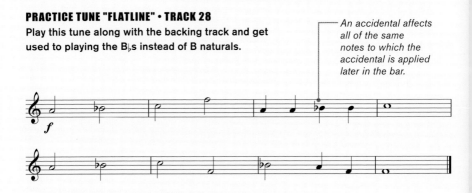

Natural notation

Notice in the third bar that the second B isn't marked as either a flat or natural. The rule is that any "accidental" (sharp or flat) affects all the notes in that bar unless corrected with a natural—so the second B in bar 3 will be a B♭ despite not being marked as one. The flat only carries on until the end of the bar—any subsequent B♭'s in later bars need to be marked as such again.

PRACTICE TUNE "BE SHARP" • TRACK 29

This piece should help you to get used to playing F♯s instead of
F naturals. Be sure to hit the D at the end of bar 3 confidently and
hold it through bar 4—this will give the tune a rhythmic lift. The
crescendo should add interest too.

Charlie Parker
August 29, 1920–March 12, 1955

A disciple of Lester Young, alto saxophonist Charlie Parker
remains one of the great pioneers of jazz. Parker was born and
raised in Kansas and started to learn the saxophone at the age
of 11. He began gigging with local bands while still at school
and began to practice obsessively, sometimes more than
twelve hours a day—the work paid off and Parker developed a
phenomenal technique and fluency on the instrument. His
restless exploration for a personal style wasn't without its
setbacks—legend has it that at a jamming session in Kansas in
the 1930s, drummer Joe Jones was so unimpressed with the
young alto player that he launched one of his cymbals across
the stage to interrupt his solo.

In 1939 Parker moved to New York and met his creative equal in trumpeter Dizzy Gillespie.
The two young musicians went on to change the course of jazz history by pioneering a new
style of jazz called bebop. This music was characterized by blisteringly fast tempos and
complex rhythmic and harmonic ideas. Parker's sheer brilliance on the saxophone has
influenced every jazz musician who followed, and his compositions including "Billie's Bounce,"
"Yardbird Suite," and "Moose The Mooch" have become a part of the standard jazz repertoire.

A book of Parker's solos called the *Charlie Parker Omnibook* contains many Parker solos
written out and is a great introduction to his music.

Key recordings: *Charlie Parker With Strings* (1950); *Now's The Time* (box set of
various dates).

Lesson 8 • The major scale

The major scale is one of the fundamental aspects of all Western music. There are too many examples of songs in the major key to list here but by understanding the major scale and its uses you will unlock another musical concept and help your development.

Introducing the major scale

The major scale consists of a set of eight consecutive notes from a starting note (called the "root") to the same note an octave higher. Here is a C major scale.

C major

C major is the best place to start because it doesn't have any sharps or flats, so is easy both to read and understand. When you play through the scale on your saxophone, it should have a familiar, comfortable sound. Even if you didn't know what it was, you will have heard the major scale many times before—it's as important a building block to music as the alphabet is to language. Notice that the notes are numbered from 1 to 8—musicians often refer to notes by their numerical relationship to the key or the root (in this case C) and will talk about intervals of thirds, fourths, fifths etc (see page 35). This gives the notes a context and will be very helpful later on.

The important thing to notice about the scale is that it is not symmetrical. The intervals between the notes are sometimes tones (whole steps) and sometimes semitones (half steps.) Here is the scale again with the intervals marked as either tones or semitones:

Tones/semitones within the major scale

Lesson 7 introduced you to sharps and flats and the resultant intervals of tones and semitones. It's important to realize that the major scale has two in-built semitone intervals; in the case of C major between E and F and between B and C (there are no sharps/flats between E and F and B and C.) These semitone intervals are crucial to the sound of the major scale–a scale made entirely of whole tones has a very peculiar sound. In short, for a major to function it needs to have the same pattern of tones and semitones: TONE, TONE, SEMITONE, TONE, TONE, TONE, SEMITONE.

Other keys

The tone/semitone pattern works perfectly in C major without any accidentals (sharps/flats) needed, however, to make a major scale work from another starting point you might need to add accidentals. Exercise 1 shows the F major scale with no accidentals:

EXERCISE 1

Play through this exercise–notice how the B sticks out and sounds very unusual.

The gap between A and B in this example is a tone when it should be a semitone. To preserve the T T S T T T S model of C major, the distance between A and B needs to be shortened to a semitone.

EXERCISE 2

To shorten this interval, the B should become a B♭.

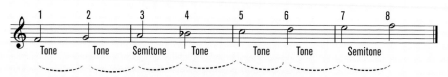

Adding the B♭ makes the scale conform to the pattern needed to make a major scale. Note that the numbers of the notes now relate to F major. The note G in C major is the fifth, but in F it is the second. The numbering system is subjective to each key rather than an absolute numbering of each note.

EXERCISE 3

Now go through the same process but with a G major scale. Firstly it's written with no accidentals at all—look through the scale and work out where the semitone intervals are and where they need to be (for a major scale, the semitone intervals are between 3 and 4 and 7 and 8). Add any sharps/flats you need to preserve this pattern.

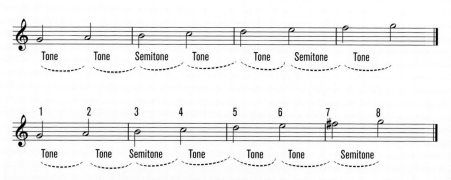

This time you need to add an F♯ to the scale to make the semitone interval between the seventh (F♯) and the eighth (G).

Key signatures

By adding sharps and flats and following the tone/semitone pattern established by C major you can create the same scale and eventually the same palette of notes and melodies but from different starting points. This is the concept of a "key." The same melody can be played from any starting point, and as long as the relationships between the notes are the same the melody will sound the same. To preserve the pattern starting on an F, all instances of B should be played as B♭, and to do the same from a G all instances of F should be played as F♯. These notes are usually given a symbol at the start of the piece called a "key signature."

EXERCISE 4

Notice the ♭ sign at the start of F major scale. The ♭ is on the B line and indicates that all Bs are to be played as flats. This saves writing a ♭ sign every time there is a B. It also gives a clue to the performer as to the key of the piece and can help with interpretation.

EXERCISE 5

Below is the scale of G major, with the sharp symbol on the F line in the key signature. This indicates that all Fs are to be played as sharps.

There are 12 key signatures in total—one for each of the 12 notes—meaning that each can be a starting point in its own right. See the Scale library on page 156 for each key and major scale written out.

Transposing between keys

As long as you preserve the tone/semitone pattern of each key by following the key signature you can play any melody from any given point and still make it sound the same.

EXERCISE 6

Here is the numerical pattern for "Mary Had A Little Lamb." See if you can play it in C major, G major, and F major by using the same pattern for each of the three keys. The notes are given for C major—see if you can work them out yourself using the numbers for G major and F major. Remember to watch out for the key signatures.

> **TOP TUNE–CLASSICAL/CONTEMPORARY**
> **Takashi Yoshimatsu "Fuzzy Bird Sonata"**
> This 1991 work by Japanese composer Takashi Yoshimatsu mixes many contemporary styles to produce a dazzling showcase for the alto saxophone.

Mary Had A Little Lamb (C Major)

Mary Had A Little Lamb (G Major)

Mary Had A Little Lamb (F major)

Play list

Try this with some other tunes—"Happy Birthday" starts with 5 5 6 5 8 7, for example. "Amazing Grace" starts with 5 1 3 2 1 3. Note that the second note of "Amazing Grace" is higher, not lower, than the first. If you can play these tunes in three different keys you will be doing great work for yourself as a musician as well as a saxophonist.

Dexter Gordon
February 27, 1923–April 25, 1990

For many, Dexter Gordon is the quintessential jazz tenor player. His husky tone, languid phrasing, and peerless interpretations of classic jazz material sum up all the iconography associated with jazz and its lifestyle. A famous photograph by Herman Leonard from 1948 shows Dexter at work in New York and captures the atmosphere of a smoky jazz club perfectly.

Dexter Gordon was born in Los Angeles and got his first big gig with Lionel Hampton's band in 1940, before ending up New York where he played and recorded with Charlie Parker and the other bebop musicians. An awesome live performer, Dexter's bebop playing ranks with the very best and his work was well documented on the Blue Note label: *Go*, *A Swinging Affair*, and *Our Man In Paris* all capture his sound and style perfectly. Dexter Gordon also starred in the 1987 film *Round Midnight* as saxophonist Dale Turner—a semi-autobiographical role.

Key recordings: *Go*, 1962; *A Swinging Affair*, 1962; *Our Man In Paris*, 1963.

Lesson 9 • Eighth-notes and sixteenth-notes

So far you've been playing music that only contains four-beat notes (whole-notes) two-beat notes (half-notes), and one-beat notes (quarter-notes). In this lesson you will learn about notes that are smaller than a beat: eighth-notes and sixteenth-notes. You will also learn about syncopation—a way of playing notes off the beat that will unlock the sound of jazz and other modern styles.

Eighth-notes

Just as a half-note is half of a whole-note and a quarter-note is half of a half-note, an eighth-note is half of a quarter-note. In the same way as the others, an eighth-note also has an equivalent rest.

EXERCISE 1

Play through this example and be sure that you are dividing the notes accurately in half each time. Set up a strong pulse with your foot (or use the second hand of a clock for a really clear tempo).

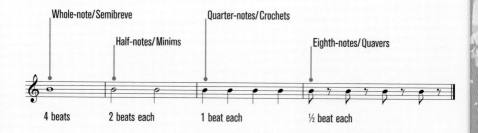

EXERCISE 2

You will notice in Exercise 1 that an eighth-note on its own sounds much like a short quarter-note. Eighth-notes come into their own when played in groups. Here are some pairs of eighth-notes—notice how they are grouped together by the "beams" across the top.

EXERCISE 3

Groups of four eighth-notes can be beamed together too:

EXERCISE 4 • TRACK 30

Using words can often help you with rhythms. Any one- and two-syllable words will help you make the change from quarter-notes to eighth-notes—here we use "tea" and "coffee."

tea   tea   tea tea   co-ffee co-ffee co-ffee co-ffee   tea tea co-ffee co-ffee   co-ffee co-ffee tea   tea

EXTRA PRACTICE

Now play through the three major scales from Lesson 8 with eighth-notes instead of quarter-notes (see pages 56–59). Try lots of different tempos and be sure to split the beat evenly into two for clear and rhythmic eighth-notes.

Sixteenth-notes

Continuing our subdivision of notes by halving an eighth-note we get a "sixteenth-note" or "semiquaver." There are four sixteenth-notes to a quarter-note, so in effect each beat has now been split into four equal parts. Below are some sixteenth-notes and sixteenth-note rests—notice how multiple notes are beamed like eighth-notes but with a double beam (see Exercise 6).

EXERCISE 5

EXERCISE 6 · TRACK 31

To help you "feel" the sixteenth-notes, repeat the four-syllable word "cappuccino" as you are tapping out the rhythm.

capp-u-ccin-o capp-u-ccin-o capp-u ccin-o capp-u-ccin-o capp-u-ccin-o capp-u-ccin-o capp-u-ccin-o capp-u-cin-o

capp-u-ccin-o capp-u-ccin-o capp-u-ccin-o capp-u-ccin-o capp-u-ccin-o capp-u-ccin-o capp-u-ccin-o capp-u-cin-o

PRACTICE TUNES

Here are some tunes to play that mix up quarter-notes, eighth-notes, and sixteenth-notes. Tap out the rhythm before attempting to play the pieces.

PRACTICE TUNE "FIGURE OF EIGHT" • TRACK 32

PRACTICE TUNE "SWEET SIXTEENTHS" • TRACK 33

PRACTICE TUNE "DOUBLING UP" • TRACK 34

Syncopation

By splitting beats into halves and quarters (using eighth-notes and sixteenth-notes), it is possible to place a note between beats. So far you have always played notes starting squarely on a beat, so it has been relatively easy to place notes on beats one, two, three, or four. Syncopation allows you to play with more rhythmic variety and to create the funky rhythms associated with jazz and other groove-based music.

Below is a line of eighth-notes followed by eighth-note rests and eighth-notes. The beat falls on the rest—the arrows show where the beats fall.

On and off-beat eighth-notes

The eighth-notes in the eighth-note and rest sequence, above, can be said to be "off-beat" eighth-notes because they fall between the four beats of the bar as opposed to "on-beat" eighth-notes that fall on the beat. Practice clapping or playing these—it can help to imagine your two-syllable eighth-note word and then miss out the first syllable.

EXERCISE 7 • Track 35

cof fee cof fee cof fee cof fee cof fee cof fee cof fee cof fee

Strong delivery

Syncopated rhythms rely on a strong, punchy delivery for their effect otherwise they can sound like incorrect on-beat notes! Use strong, definite tonguing for a clear attack.

EXERCISE 8 · TRACK 36

See if you can syncopate this line by halving each beat and playing the second eighth-note off the beat. All the notes shown below are on the beat.

EXERCISE 9

This is how Exercise 7 might look, syncopated. See if you can move each note forward by half a beat to make this "riff" more funky! (As shown in Exercise 10, below.)

EXERCISE 10 · TRACK 37

EXERCISE 11 · TRACK 38
You can also mix up on- and off-beat notes (see also Exercise 12).

EXERCISE 12 · TRACK 39

PRACTICE TUNE "OFF BEAT, ON SONG"
This is essentially the same as "Doubling Up" on page 65, but
with a few syncopations. The eighth-note rests really liven up the
piece and make it groove a bit more.

TOP TUNE–JAZZ
John Coltrane
"Giant Steps"
The title track of
Coltrane's 1960 album,
"Giant Steps" features a
labyrinthine chord
progression that still
challenges aspiring
saxophone players today.

Paul Desmond
November 25, 1924–May 30, 1977

PLAYER PROFILE

Much of the groundbreaking music of the 1940s centered around New York and the bebop style; however there was a very different sound emerging on the West Coast of the United States—in particular, in Los Angeles and San Francisco. West Coast jazz or "cool" jazz borrowed heavily from bebop but added a lighter and more airy approach to the music than its fiery New York cousin. Cool jazz focused more on melody and atmosphere than the complex harmonic invention of bebop. Alto saxophonist Paul Desmond was a key figure in the cool jazz music scene—his beautifully delicate and refined alto sound was said to sound like a sea breeze through the palm trees, and Desmond himself said he was trying to capture the sound of a dry martini. Most famous for his work with the great pianist Dave Brubeck, Paul Desmond has achieved musical immortality for his playing on "Take Five" from Brubeck's 1959 album *Time Out*.

Paul Desmond also collaborated with other West Coast musicians—baritone saxophonist Gerry Mulligan and trumpeter/vocalist Chet Baker—to produce beautiful, melodic jazz of the highest class.

Key recordings: *Time Out* with **Dave Brubeck Quartet, 1959;** *Two Of A Mind* with **Gerry Mulligan, 1962;** *Easy Living*, **1963.**

Lesson 10 • Straight, swung, and dotted eighth-notes

Lesson 9 introduced eighth-notes and sixteenth-notes and some of their uses in contemporary saxophone playing. Hopefully you are now really comfortable with on- and off-beat notes and using syncopation to give your playing a really funky edge!

> **TOP TUNE–JAZZ**
> Cannonball Adderley
> "All Blues" with Miles Davis
> The alto saxophone on *Kind Of Blue* (1959), Julian "Cannonball" Adderley added a bubbly, bluesy, joyful sound to Davis' most celebrated album.

Straight and swung eighth-notes

In this lesson you will discover how to "swing" your eighth-notes. Swung eighth-notes are common in jazz music and by learning how to swing eighth-notes you will be able to "jazz up" any melody.

Previously we have treated eighth-notes as even—a quarter-note split equally into two halves to produce two notes of equal length. Swung eighth-notes change the length of the eighth-notes and make the first one longer than the second. To do this we are first going to split a quarter-note into three equal parts called "triplets." The easiest way to think of this is to use a three-syllable word, such as "banana."

EXERCISE 1 • TRACK 40
Play through Exercise 1 on your saxophone and try to be really accurate as you divide the quarter-note into three equal parts—you'll need to tongue the triplets to separate them.

EXERCISE 2 · TRACK 41

Swung eighth-notes are derived from triplets—all you need to do is to join the first two together to make one longer note. You will then end up with two notes of different lengths that take up one beat.

The second syllable of the word "banana" now becomes silent but try to hear or feel it as you play the swung eighth-notes. This evolution of triplets into two unequal note lengths is the origin of swung or "jazz" eighth-notes. They are usually written as ordinary eighth-notes but with an instruction at the top of the page that reads "swing."

PRACTICE TUNE "TO SWING OR NOT TO SWING" · TRACK 42

Play through the next piece twice—firstly with even or "straight" eighth-notes, then again with swung eighth-notes. Without any accompaniment on the track you will clearly hear the difference between straight and swung eighth-notes, which will prepare you for some of the jazz pieces later in the book.

Dotted quarter-notes and eighth-notes

In Lesson 5 you learned how to increase a note by half of
its value again by putting a dot next to it—a dotted half-note
became a three-beat note, for example (see Lesson 5 on
page 41 if you need a recap).

The same principle applies to quarter-notes and eighth-
notes—both can be lengthened by a half to make a one-and-a-
half-beat note (dotted quarter-note) and a three-quarter-length
note (dotted eighth-note.)

EXERCISE 3

Play through this simple rhythmic pattern up and down the G major
scale (and F major and C major if you want some practice). To create
a dotted quarter-note simply join the first and second notes of this
pattern together.

EXERCISE 4 · TRACK 43

The first of the pair of eighth-notes in the below phrase has now been
added onto the quarter-note to make one longer note of one-and-a-half
beats. Play through this a few times until you are really comfortable
placing the second eighth-note after the beat.

EXERCISE 5

Exercises 4 and 5 sound exactly the same—note that the dotted quarter-
note is just another way of writing a quarter-note tied to an eighth-note.

EXERCISE 6 • TRACK 44

Dotted eighth-notes work in the same way as dotted half-notes and quarter-notes. A dotted eighth-note becomes worth three-quarters of a beat or the equivalent of three sixteenth-notes. Often a dotted eighth-note is followed by a sixteenth-note.

You'll notice that dotted eighth-notes sound very similar to swung eighth-notes, but with swung eighth-notes the second note (the shorter one) is slightly longer than a sixteenth-note (a third of the beat as opposed to a quarter). Be careful not to make the second note of a pair of swung eighth-notes too short as this will produce a clipped, jerky sound rather than the languid, smooth-sounding jazz eighth-notes. Play the backing tracks for Exercises 2 and 6 and listen to the difference between swung and dotted eighth-notes.

Repeat marks

If you wish to indicate that a section is to be repeated you can add "repeat marks"–these are double bar lines with double dots. The sections between these double bars are to be repeated. Just the dotted double bar lines and dots indicate one repeat. To add more repeats, simply write how many times the section is to be repeated.

Repeat marks

PRACTICE TUNE "SWINGIN' TIME" • TRACK 45

This is a simple jazz tune that includes both swung eighth-notes and dotted notes—play along with the backing track and try to make the eighth-notes really swing. Remember to use your three-syllable word if in doubt to help with the rhythm.

Lesson 11 • Minor keys and scales

Major keys and scales are used to create satisfying, happy-sounding music. The opposite of the major scale is the minor scale. The minor key and its associated scales are used to express the darker, sadder side of music. The minor key is as important to music as the major keys we explored in Lesson 8 (see page 56) and again is probably familiar to you even if you don't know it yet!

Introducing the minor scale

The most important difference between major and minor is the third note. Lesson 8 looked at the tone and semitone intervals between the notes in a major scale—the interval between the second and third notes is always a tone, creating a bright interval between the root and the third. The minor key has an interval of a semitone between the second and third, and this dramatically changes the mood of the scale. You will need E♭ (below) for Exercise 1 (opposite).

Fingering for D♯/E♭

To play E♭ or D♯, finger a normal D and then add your right-hand fourth finger to the key underneath. Note that this key is split into two halves with a roller—for E♭/D♯ use the top half. As with the other low register notes, simply add the octave key to transfer up an octave.

EXERCISE 1A

Play through Exercises 1a and 1b and notice the effect of flattening the third (in this case the E as we are in the key of C).

EXERCISE 1B · TRACK 46

The new interval created between the root note (C) and the flattened third (E♭) is called a minor third.

Major to minor melodies

Now try to transfer a melody in the major key to a minor key. Start with the tunes you played in Lesson 8 (see page 60). Any time there is a third, change it to a minor third. So if you are playing the tunes in C major, replace any Es with E♭s. The results are often amusing since the mood of the song changes totally—"Mary Had A Little Lamb" sounds very different from the usual soothing nursery rhyme and "Amazing Grace" loses some of its uplifting nature.

The flattening of the third is the most fundamental characteristic of minor keys. To qualify as minor, the third must be flattened. There are, however, lots of variations in minor keys—the two most common are the "melodic minor" and the "harmonic minor."

Melodic minor

As the name suggests, the melodic minor scale is to do with melody, and it is also different in its ascending and descending forms, which makes it tricky to play at first. We have already covered the ascending part of the scale—it is simply the minor in its most basic form: a flattened third but no other differences to the major scale.

EXERCISE 2A

Play through the scale again but this time stop on the B natural.

Leaving the B hanging like this creates a sense of unrest and tension. The seventh note wants to pull up to the safety of the root to complete the phrase.

John Coltrane

September 23, 1926–July 17, 1967

The most influential tenor saxophonist since Coleman Hawkins, John Coltrane's huge body of work from the 1950s and '60s redefined the sound of both the saxophone and modern jazz. Like many musicians of the time, Coltrane learned his trade in high school and military bands. In 1955 Coltrane was called by Miles Davis to join his new quintet and he moved to New York to take up the offer. Coltrane's robust, angular saxophone playing provided the perfect contrast to Miles Davis' cool lyricism and the quintet was one of the most successful jazz groups of all time. The four albums *Cookin'* (1956), *Relaxin'* (1957), *Workin'* (1959), and *Steamin'* (1961) capture the work of the quintet at their creative peak. Coltrane also participated in Miles Davis' celebrated masterpiece *Kind Of Blue* in 1959.

Coltrane left Davis and in 1960 formed his own quartet where his music became exploratory and technically complex—his tune "Giant Steps" is still considered a landmark tune for aspiring jazz musicians. He also pioneered the use of the soprano saxophone in modern jazz in his reworking of "My Favorite Things" in 1961.

Coltrane's work in the 1960s culminated in his staggering 1965 album *A Love Supreme*, an expression of Coltrane's religious faith.

Key recordings: *Blue Train*, 1957; *Kind Of Blue* (with Miles Davis) 1959; *Giant Steps* (1959); *A Love Supreme*, 1965.

EXERCISE 2B

Now play Exercise 2b and allow the tension to be resolved by ending the phrase with a C. This "pull" toward the root is great for ascending minor tunes but isn't so good for descending lines as they contradict the upward pull of the scale. The descending melodic minor cancels out the bright seventh note by flattening it as well as flattening the sixth. This creates two intervals of a tone on the way down the scale.

Fingering for C♯/D♭

This is possibly the easiest fingering on the saxophone, since it involves no fingers at all. Your left thumb should be in place on the black pad as usual (press the octave key for high C♯) and keep your fingers poised above the keys. C♯ can sound a little bit thin at first—try to copy the sound quality of your lower notes to C♯.

EXERCISE 3

Now play Exercise 2b and Exercise 3 together to create a C melodic minor scale.

Fingering for G♯/A♭

To play G♯/A♭, add your left-hand little finger to a G natural fingering. The square pad by your left little finger operates four notes—all the keys are connected by rollers, much like the key played by the fourth finger when playing low E♭. This allows you to move smoothly between the keys. G♯/A♭ is the thin key at the top of the pad.

PRACTICE TUNE "MELODIC MINOR ETUDE" • TRACK 47

This is a classical-style solo piece that explores the sound of the melodic minor scale. Try to make the piece sound elegant and serene.

Try to play the "Melodic Minor Etude" in other keys—if in doubt about how to transpose, look at the minor scales in the Scale library (see page 156).

Harmonic minor

The harmonic minor keeps the bright, unflattened
seventh of the ascending melodic minor but also has
the flattened sixth of the descending melodic minor.

EXERCISE 4 • TRACK 48

The harmonic minor has a very different sound to the
melodic minor. The big jump between the A♭ and the
B gives the scale an Arabic/Egyptian feel.

PRACTICE TUNE "HARMONIC MINOR ETUDE" • TRACK 49

This piece is similar in style to the "Melodic Minor
Etude" (opposite) but explores the sound of the harmonic
minor. Notice the use of A♭ and B and the distinct sound
they create.

Minor key signatures

With so many variations in minor keys it can be confusing to decide on a key signature for the minor key. The descending melodic minor scale has the most alterations to the major scale so these are all put into the key signature. C minor, for example, has B♭, E♭, and A♭, and so these are all put into the key signature. The altered notes on the way up are then written as naturals (A natural and B natural). Interestingly, the very bright B natural in D minor that has been highlighted as an important part of the minor sound isn't written in the key signature but as an alteration.

EXERCISE 6

Try to play through the following scales in minor keys—both the melodic and harmonic forms of the scales are featured, as well as the key signatures.

G melodic minor

G harmonic minor

EXERCISE 7

A full set of minor scales can be found in the Scale library (see pages 156–211). Always make sure you check the key signature as the character of the scale is defined by the sharps and flats.

D melodic minor

D harmonic minor

Listening

The minor key is as omnipresent in music as the major—
whatever your taste in music there will be use of the minor
key. The Etude pieces in this lesson have a classical feel
reminiscent of J. S. Bach. Bach didn't write for the saxophone
because it hadn't been invented in his time (see page 12),
however, try listening to the Bach "Flute Sonatas"—if you enjoy
these you can play them on the saxophone, since many have
been transcribed for the saxophone.

"Yesterday" by The Beatles features a strong melodic minor
line—listen to the line "all my troubles seemed so far away" and
you should hear a melodic minor scale. (It starts on the fifth of
the melodic minor and runs up to the minor third above).

We will further explore minor scales and their relationship to
major scales in Lessons 12 and 13.

STAN GETZ
February 2, 1927–June 6, 1991

An avid disciple of Lester Young, tenor saxophone man Stan
Getz's silky smooth tone and lyrical playing earned him the
nickname "The Sound." At the tender age of 15, after learning
the saxophone during his school years, Stan Getz went on the
road with trombonist and band leader Jack Teagarden's group.
In 1947 Getz joined the legendary Woody Herman band as
a featured soloist and completed a stellar saxophone section
along with Serge Chaloff, Zoot Simms, and Herbie Steward.

In the 1950s Getz recorded numerous albums with the big
jazz names of the day including Dizzy Gillespie and Oscar
Peterson. In 1964 he had his biggest hit with the album *Getz/
Gilberto*, an effortless mix of jazz and Brazilian bossa nova.

Stan Getz changed direction in the 1970s and turned his
hand to jazz fusion with pianist/keyboard player Chick Corea's
band but returned to acoustic jazz in the 1980s where he co-led a quartet with pianist Kenny
Barron. The band played fluent melodic jazz of the highest class and were a huge draw on the
international jazz circuit.

Stan Getz's purity of sound and faultless control of melody and interpretation have made
him a role model for many aspiring saxophone players.

Key recordings: *Stan Getz and the Oscar Peterson Trio*, 1957; *Getz/Gilberto*, 1964.

Lesson 12 •
Chords and arpeggios

Lessons 8 and 11 introduced major and minor scales. Now you are now familiar with the sound of these scales and their importance to music as building blocks for melodies. In this lesson we will explore scales as a source of chords and arpeggios.

Introducing chords and arpeggios

Let's return to the G major scale. If we play the notes from 1 to 8 we get a satisfying and by now familiar-sounding scale. However, if all the notes were played together the result wouldn't be so good. The notes are too close together for the ear to separate. To make a "chord" (a group of notes played simultaneously) you would play the root note (G in this case) the third (B) and fifth (D). By leaving this space between the notes, the ear can hear the separate notes more easily and recognize the major or minor sound.

Chords are played on instruments where it's possible to play more than one note at a time—piano and guitar are the most common, but harp, accordion, and various percussion instruments also play chords. The saxophone is a single-line instrument (i.e. can play only one note at once) and so cannot play chords, however, to create a similar effect to a chord the saxophone and other single-line instruments play "arpeggios." Arpeggio means "broken chord" in Italian and allows melody instruments to outline chords. By playing the root, third, and fifth notes of the scale you can simulate a chord (known as a triad).

EXERCISE 1

Play Exercise 1 and hear how effectively the arpeggio outlines the key
(the chord at the end is impossible on the saxophone).

Major and minor arpeggios

Just like scales, arpeggios can be major or minor. The important note
is the third because it carries the quality of the key and determines
whether it is major or minor.

EXERCISE 2

Here is a G minor arpeggio—by lowering the B to a B♭, the key changes
from major to minor.

EXERCISE 3

Here are some more major and minor arpeggios (see the Scale library
on page 156 for a full set of major and minor arpeggios in each key).

C major/minor arpeggios

D major/minor arpeggios

F major/minor arpeggios

Melody and accompaniment

So far this book has focused on single-line melodies. As a saxophonist you will nearly always be playing the melody—the tune—and for many people the most memorable part of a piece of music. By introducing chords, we are starting to look at another aspect of music: the accompaniment. Underneath the melody, an accompaniment serves to give the music context and a sympathetic base from which the melody can function. Different accompaniments can affect the melody in different ways. This will be further explored later in the book, and although the saxophone is often the melody instrument and not always involved in the accompaniment, it is important for you to have a grasp of the role of chords and accompaniment.

"Sundowner"

This is a jaunty calypso-style piece that layers three parts on top of each other to "spell out" the chords of the piece. By playing the three parts, you will get a feel for playing both melody and accompaniment parts.

The piece starts with a bass line that uses arpeggios to outline the three main chords of the tune: G, C, and D majors. The pattern of the bass line is the same for each chord—the G, B, and D are the arpeggio of the G major, moving to the arpeggio of C major (C, E, and G) and the D, F♯, and A are the arpeggio of D major.

The middle part is an accompaniment to the bass line that spells out the chords by weaving through the G major scale and picks out some of the arpeggio notes.

The top line is the melody—as you play it, notice how it sits on top of the other two parts.

TOP TUNE—FILM/TV
Terry Harrington—The Simpsons
theme with Danny Elfman
Film composer Danny Elfman wrote this catchy theme in 1989. Saxophone-mad Lisa Simpson's solos are played by session musician Terry Harrington and are often different—listen out for all the improvised solos in the main theme.

PRACTICE TUNE "SUNDOWNER" • TRACK 50

Use the backing track to play this tune—the track incorporates all three
parts on various instruments. Mix and match the different parts and see
how it feels to play melody, accompaniment, and bass parts.

"Prelude in A minor"

This is another multilayered piece that uses arpeggios to spell out
the chords. The style and mood of this piece are very different to
"Sundowner" on page 85. The piece is in a minor key (A minor) and is
based around the use of the A minor scale and arpeggio. The use of
the minor key gives this piece a sadder, more forlorn sound. The piece
uses other arpeggios too to provide some movement and interest in
the accompaniment—see if you can identify other arpeggios in the
piece and ask yourself if they are major or minor.

PRACTICE TUNE "PRELUDE IN A MINOR" • TRACK 51

Use the backing track to play this tune—the track incorporates all three
parts on various instruments. Practice the different parts and see how it
feels to play melody, accompaniment, and bass parts.

Lesson 13 •
Chord progression

In this lesson you will learn how to build a triad (three-note chord) from each degree of the major scale. This will give you a set of chords that are all relevant or "diatonic" to the key in question, i.e. chords that contain only the notes of that key and no accidentals. You will also discover how to use this palette of chords to create satisfying chord sequences and play some music in different styles using only the chords of the key—this will unlock basic chord sequences and give you a greater understanding of how music is put together.

Building a triad

Firstly, let's build a three-note chord from each degree of the C major scale. Notice how each note is labeled with a roman numeral—this represents the notes' relationship to the root or tonic of the key. Familiarize yourself with this use of roman numerals as it is a very common way of describing chords within a chord progression. Musicians will refer to a "III chord" or a "IV, V, I" to describe what will happen in the chord sequence. This allows you to learn a chord sequence as an abstract idea and then apply it to a key of your choice, allowing you greater flexibility (see page 60).

C major chords: Roots and fifths

So far we have only the root note of each of our seven "diatonic"
chords in C major. Let's start by adding the fifth of each—to do
this you must simply count five notes up from the note in question
and add that note.

Notice how all of the fifths are also notes from the C major
scale—i.e. there are no sharps or flats.

C major chords: Roots, thirds, and fifths

Next we'll add the third to complete the triad. In the same way as
you counted five notes from the root to find the fifth, you should
count up three notes from the root to find the third.

Major and minor thirds

Look back to Lessons 8, 11, and 12 and you will remember that the third has a particular importance within a key because it tells us whether the key is major or minor. Nearly all music is in a major or minor key and the tonality of major or minor dramatically affects the mood of the music.

Within the seven diatonic chords of each major key there is a mixture of major and minor chords, giving variety to the palette of chords and allowing different moods to be created without altering the key itself. For the chords to remain diatonic to C major they mustn't contain any sharps or flats—this will naturally create major and minor thirds over certain chords. The way to tell (apart from hearing the sound) is to look at the distance between root and third notes—if it is four semitones from the root to the third then the interval is major. If it is three semitones then the interval is minor.

EXERCISE 1

Play each of these triads one note at a time to familiarize yourself with the sound of major and minor chords within the key.

There are many pieces of music that use this set of chords to make coherent chord progressions. From early classical composers such as Bach and Handel to bands like The Beatles and U2, these chords are used to form the basis of many compositions.

Pachelbel's "Canon in D"

Johann Pachelbel (1653–1706) was a German composer and organist. His most popular piece is the "Canon in D" that features on many classical music compilations. The "Canon in D" features a repeated bass line, which we will use as the basis for Exercise 2.

EXERCISE 2

First, play through the sequence below and see if it sounds familiar. It is the bass line for the "Canon in D."

EXERCISE 3

Next see if you can add the third and the fifth to each chord to create a triad for each chord (remember only to use the notes of C major so don't include any sharps or flats). Play the chords, again one note at a time. Identify which chords are major and which are minor (refer back to Exercise 1 and check against the roman numerals if necessary).

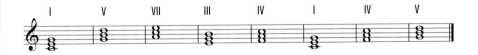

EXERCISE 4 · TRACK 52

Play through these examples until you are comfortable with each.
Now start to pick and choose which notes and rhythms you play
over each chord—use the backing track and start to make your
own lines over the chord sequence. Remember that any notes
from C major will "fit," however, some sound better than others at
certain times. Each chord has three notes (root, third, and fifth)
that will sound really strong—start by using these and then try to
thread them together.

EXERCISE 4A

EXERCISE 4B

EXERCISE 4C

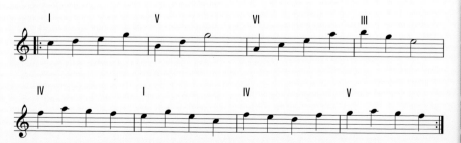

Other tunes using diatonic chords

There are many examples of tunes in all genres of music whose melodies are built on diatonic chords. A contrasting set of tunes for you to practice is introduced on the following pages. In each case, only the chord sequence is given—see if you can fill in the melody yourself.

EXERCISE 5

"Let It Be" by The Beatles uses diatonic chords to make a sequence. This time we will play in the key of G major but all the same principles will apply. Here are the chords diatonic to G major. Although the chords themselves are different, notice that the quality of the chords (major or minor) correspond in the same way to those of C major in that chords I, IV, and V are major and II, III, VI, and VII are always minor (see page 90). Note that major chords are shown by letter name only, and minor chords feature a letter "m."

EXERCISE 6

Here is the chord sequence to "Let It Be" as roman numerals—see if you can fill out both the chord name and the type.

"LET IT BE" • TRACK 53

Although the style and melody of "Let It Be" is totally
different to Pachelbel's "Canon in D," you should be able
to hear the similarities between the chord sequences.

Here is a chord sequence similar to "Let It Be" with
verses and chorus marked. See if you can work out the
melody for yourself—it starts on a D. Note the use of
repeats—each line is repeated. The arrangement on the
backing track runs as follows: verse 1, verse 2, chorus 1,
chorus 2, verse 3, verse 4, chorus 3, chorus 4. Once you
are comfortable playing the tune, experiment with your
own variations—try to embellish the melody and add your
own flourishes.

Kings of melody
Paul McCartney (left)
and John Lennon
performing with The
Beatles during the
group's final world
tour in July 1966.

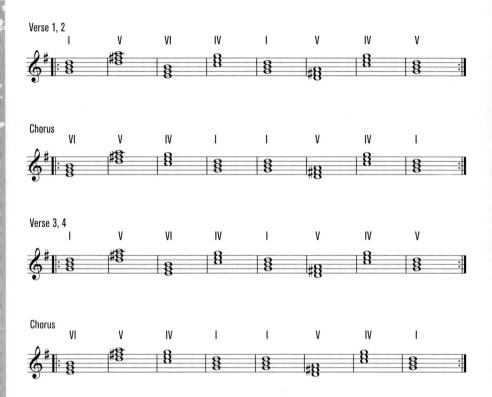

"SOMEWHERE OVER THE RAINBOW" • TRACK 54

Originally written for *The Wizard of Oz*, Harold Arlen's beautiful song
has become a classic, interpreted by many singers and musicians.
This is another song based around the diatonic chords of the key—
below is the chord sequence, this time in F major. As with "Let It
Be," see if you can work out the melody (starting on F) and play it
along with the backing track.

"ONE LOVE" • TRACK 55

The last tune in this lesson transfers diatonic chord theory to
another setting: reggae. Made famous by Bob Marley, "One Love" is
a classic reggae tune capturing the mood of the Caribbean. Again
just the chord sequence is provided for you—work out the melody by
ear. It starts on the third note of the scale, in this case E.

You should now have a good understanding of the uses of chords
I, II, III, IV, V, VI, and VII. Whenever you are learning a new chord
sequence, remember to arpeggiate each chord by playing each of
the three notes individually to spell out the chord.

Use the songs and backing tracks to learn the melodies suggested
as well as trying out your own variations and embellishments.

We're jammin'
Bob Marley performing live at
The Rainbow Theatre in London,
June 1977.

Lesson 14 • The blues

The distinct sound of the blues has shaped the popular music of the twentieth century. From its humble beginnings as American folk music there are very few genres of popular music that can't in some way be traced back to the blues–rock, R 'n' B, hip hop, jazz, and soul all owe part of their sound to the blues.

Playing the blues

The blues originated in the American Deep South and are a mix of folk songs, spirituals, and work songs that were popular at the time. Music legends such as W. C. Handy, Robert Johnson, and Bessie Smith are among the early pioneers.

The blues is generally a sad music, and as we've already discovered in Lesson 11 (see page 74), to create a melancholy effect you need to add a touch of the minor sound. In this chapter we will create a blues scale and use this as a template for tunes and solos in a bluesy style.

Maceo Parker
February 14, 1943–

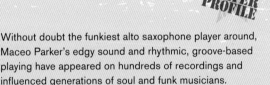

PLAYER PROFILE

Without doubt the funkiest alto saxophone player around, Maceo Parker's edgy sound and rhythmic, groove-based playing have appeared on hundreds of recordings and influenced generations of soul and funk musicians.

Parker's big break came in the mid-1960s when James Brown happened across a late-night club gig in North Carolina featuring Maceo and his drummer brother Melvin–Brown was so knocked out by the pair that he offered them a gig with his band. Parker's contribution to James Brown's music was huge–the saxophone break on "I Feel Good" has inspired alto sax players the world over.

In the 1970s Parker joined funk bands Funkadelic and Parliament, and since the 1990s he has toured with his own band. This high-energy show really comes into its own live–the storming shows regularly run for three hours or more and are guaranteed to get you moving!

Key recordings: "I Feel Good" with James Brown (1965); *Parliament's Mothership Connection***, 1976;** *Made By Maceo***, 2003.**

The major scale and "blue notes"

The early blues songs were based in a major key, however
to add expression and mood to the songs, certain notes
were flattened to give the songs a minor feel (remember
how you flattened the third to create a minor arpeggio
in Lesson 12, see page 83). This idea of flattening or
"minorizing" a major sound is continued in the blues scale
by flattening the fifth and the seventh. The result is a six-note
scale somewhere between a scale and arpeggio.

EXERCISE 1 • TRACK 56

Play through the G blues scale and notice the effect that the flattened notes
have on the overall sound—notice how the "blue" notes (B^b, D^b, and F) clash
with the major scale (see Lesson 8). This is intentional and an important
part of the blues sound, but may take you a while to adapt to. See the Scale
library on pages 156–211 for blues scales in the other keys.

EXERCISE 2 • TRACK 57

This is a simple blues-style tune that uses the blues scale and "blue"
notes. The notes marked with an arrow are the blue notes and are the
flattened versions of the major notes. Each of these should be given a
little extra emphasis to make them sound as earthy and bluesy as
possible. Make sure that you swing the eighth-notes too (see Lesson
10)—this will give the tune the right rhythmic feel. Concentrate on
making the piece smooth and rhythmic—if you can swing on your own
you will sound fantastic when playing with the backing band. Make sure
the rests are the correct length too.

Twelve-bar blues

The twelve-bar blues is the most common blues form,
and as the name suggests, consists of a twelve-bar
sequence that loops round and round. The sequence is
built on three chords: I, IV, and V.

EXERCISE 3 · TRACK 58

Here is a twelve-bar blues in G:

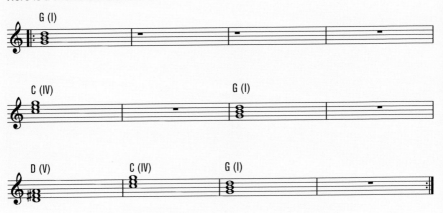

This is the most common formation of twelve-bar blues—notice how it's
split into three sections of four bars' length. This will become obvious
when we add a melody and lyrics to the blues.

TOP TUNE–JAZZ
Stan Getz
"Girl from Ipanema"
This beautiful mix of
Brazilian bossa nova
and jazz from 1963 has
become a classic. Getz's
breathy tenor
saxophone and Astrud
Gilberto's vocals blend
perfectly to produce a
timeless sound.

EXERCISE 4 • TRACK 58

This is a blues-type tune with lyrics written below the notes. Notice how the first two lines are the same while the third acts as a concluding phrase. Play through the tune with the backing track.

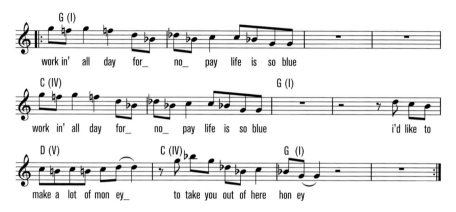

This tune is composed of notes from the blues scale—the only exceptions are the B naturals at the start of the third line (the major third). You could flatten these to a B♭ and keep the bluesy sound. Try both and see which you prefer.

The chord numbers are also included—the sequence of I, IV, and V chords is the same for all twelve-bar blues tunes so start to familiarize yourself with the chord changes. You won't always be in G, so try to think of the roman numerals and then relate them to other keys.

Your turn

Try to compose your own blues tune to play over Track 58. You should use only the notes of the G blues scale—this set of notes will certainly help you to capture the mood. You could start with the lyrics and fit the melody around them or vice versa—then play your tune over the backing.

Lesson 15 • Adding the seventh

So far all the chords we've used have contained three notes—the root, third, and the fifth. In this lesson we are going to add a fourth note to add more color and variety to our chords. The easiest way to do this is to revisit Exercise 1 in Lesson 13 (see page 90) and add an extra note to each of the seven chords we used there.

EXERCISE 1

This exercise features the seven major/minor chords that are found in the key of C major. Listen to the chords played on the piano—hearing the notes together allows you to try each note of the chord on the saxophone.

EXERCISE 2 • TRACK 59

Adding the seventh to each of these chords gives each chord a different character:

By adding the seventh note to each chord we have created three main chord types—Major 7, Minor 7, and 7. (The B minor chord has a flattened fifth and creates a different chord that we will explore later.) The minor seventh and seventh chords have a whole tone interval between the seventh and the root. Look at the D minor seventh chord, for example. The distance between the C and the D is a whole tone, whereas the major seventh chord has only a semitone interval—the C major seventh chord has only a semitone between the B and the C.

EXERCISE 3

Here are the three main chord types built from the same root:

The differences between each chord are small but significant—be sure to play the correct sharps and flats. The difference between the major seventh (B) and flattened seventh (B♭) in particular has a huge impact on the sound of the chord. Be sure in your mind of the difference between major seventh (often written maj7) and seventh chords (see above).

TOP TUNE–CLASSICAL/CONTEMPORARY
Phil Woods "Three Improvisations"
This piece for saxophone quartet stretches the possibilities of the ensemble in a unique blend of jazz and contemporary music.

PRACTICE TUNE "DREAMING" • TRACK 60

This is a soft, calm piece based around major seventh chords. The accompaniment is featured as well as the melody because this clearly spells out the chords of this piece. Notice how the accompaniment pattern spells out each chord by playing the root, third, fifth, and major seventh of each chord. You should try to make the melody soar over the accompaniment—let the long notes ring out and show off your tone.

PRACTICE TUNE "NEW ORLEANS PARADE" • TRACK 61

This New Orleans-style jazz tune demonstrates the use of seventh chords. Again the accompaniment part is included for you to play. The accompaniment is a typical traditional jazz bass line that plays the root and fifth of the chord on the first and third beats of the bar. This steady constant line gives the tune its groove.

First- and second-time bars

The brackets marked "1" and "2" in the second and third lines of "New Orleans Parade" are called first- and second-time bars. These are used when there is a repeat with a different ending. Notice that on the repeat the first four bars are the same, but the tune changes. On the first time through, play the section marked with a 1, and on the second time skip this section and head straight to the section marked 2.

PRACTICE TUNE "MINOR MINUTE" • TRACK 62

This is a tune featuring minor seventh chords. The accompaniment features the minor seventh chords played with a repeating rhythm. The minor seventh chords are included so you can play along with the accompaniment on the backing track. The melody is fairly simple and is based around the fifth, flattened seventh, and root notes, giving it a strong minor seventh sound.

Major seventh, minor seventh, and seventh chords are very common in many different types of music. You should now be familiar with their sound and some of their uses in melody and accompaniment.

Lesson 16 •
Minor pentatonic scales

As the name suggests, a pentatonic scale is a five-note scale. The pentatonic scale is present in many musical cultures including ancient Gregorian plainchant (a simple style of song associated with medieval church music), Celtic and American folk music, and Chinese music as well as contemporary rock and jazz styles. This lesson will introduce you to the minor pentatonic scale and some of its uses.

Introducing the minor pentatonic scale

The minor pentatonic has the essential notes for a defined minor sound and its simplicity and effectiveness have made it popular with melody writers all over the world.

EXERCISE 1 • TRACK 63

The minor pentatonic scale is made up of the root, $\flat$3, 4, 5, and $\flat$7 degrees of the scale. Below is the A minor pentatonic scale—practice playing this through.

Root $\flat$7   4   5 $\flat$7   Root

You may notice that the pentatonic scale is similar to the blues scale (see Lesson 14), but without the characteristic flattened fifth of the blues scale. The result is an open-sounding scale that can be easily molded to suit many different styles.

TOP TUNE–POP/FUNK/SOUL
Phil Woods "Just The Way You Are" with Billy Joel
The saxophone solo on this beautiful Billy Joel recording is one of the most famous and imitated pop saxophone solos of all time.

EXERCISE 2

This is a simple pentatonic melody, which has been written to sound like a piece of plainchant. Plainchant creates an atmosphere of calm simplicity—try to convey this as you play the melody.

Call and response

Call and response is a simple music technique involving a repeated idea (a call) and an answering phrase (response). Often the call is the same and the responses vary.

EXERCISE 3 • TRACK 64

Using the pentatonic chant, compose some of your own responses using the pentatonic scale by playing along with the backing track and try to make your own responses to the repeated call.

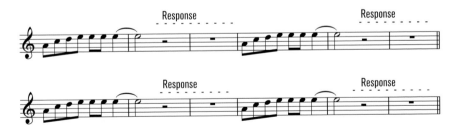

Use the A minor pentatonic scale in Exercise 1 for your note selection—this should help you capture the mood of the pentatonic sound. If you are stuck for ideas start by using the melody of the pentatonic chant (Exercise 2) as your response, then change the rhythms and notes as you see fit to create the music you want to play.

EXERCISE 4

The practice tune on the following page uses three different chords and their minor pentatonic scales—D minor, G minor, and A minor. Below are the three scales to help you. Notice that the three scales have notes in common that appear throughout the piece.

Jan Garbarek
4 March 1947–

Norwegian tenor and soprano saxophonist Jan Garbarek has forged a highly personal sound and approach to saxophone playing and composition in a long and varied career. A huge devotee of John Coltrane's playing, Garbarek developed an edgy, metallic tone similar to his idol, but concentrated on a smoother, more melodic playing style than Coltrane's.

Garbarek came to attention on the world stage during his stint with pianist Keith Jarrett's European Quartet in the 1970s—the albums *Belonging* in 1974 and *My Song* in 1977 capture the group's sound beautifully. The group was an early example of European jazz and its efforts to forge an identity away from its American roots. While owing a huge debt to jazz, the European sound is far removed from gospel, blues, and swing—the traditional roots of jazz—and instead uses European folk melodies to create a cultural identity of its own.

Garbarek has continued to explore a wide variety of musical styles and placed his lyrical playing in a series of unlikely settings—his album *Officium* features saxophone playing over Gregorian plainchant, an unlikely combination but a huge commercial and artistic success.

Key recordings: *My Song* with Keith Jarrett European Quartet, 1977; *Officium*, 1994.

PRACTICE TUNE "THE TONIC" • TRACK 65

This tune is based around the pentatonic scale. This time the style of the piece isn't a calming, reflective plainchant but a funky, soul-style piece. Look back to the syncopation featured in Lesson 9 to get an idea of how to approach this piece. The delivery needs to be punchy and rhythmic to capture the groove of the piece.

Use the pieces in this lesson to familiarize yourself with the sound of the minor pentatonic scale and its place in many different styles of music.

Lesson 17 •
Major pentatonic scales

The major pentatonic scale is very similar to the minor pentatonic scale that we explored in the previous lesson. Much like normal scales, the major and minor pentatonics can be used to suggest major and minor keys.

Introducing the major pentatonic scale

Lesson 11 explained how to find the relative minor key of a major (a minor key that shares its key signature with a major). Pentatonic scales also utilize this relationship between major and minor keys.

EXERCISE 1

In Lesson 16 we created a minor pentatonic scale using the root, ♭3, 4, 5, and ♭7. To create a major pentatonic you simply move the starting note to the relative major—in this case C. Playing the A minor pentatonic scale from a C gives you a major-sounding scale, this time using the root, 2, 3, 5, and 6.

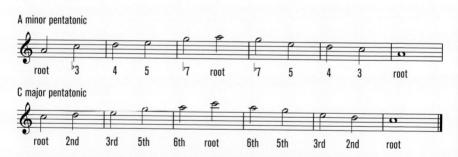

Much like a relative major scale, changing the starting note and therefore the context of the pentatonic creates a very different-sounding scale. The major pentatonic sounds bright compared to the minor. Notice also that the major pentatonic is built slightly differently—1, 2, 3, 5, 6 is different to the 1, ♭3, 4, 5, ♭7 make-up of the minor scale.

PRACTICE TUNE "THE BIRDS IN THE TREES" • TRACK 66

This is a simple folk-type melody to help you find your way around the
C major pentatonic. Notice how different it sounds from the pentatonic
chant in Lesson 16 (Exercise 2). By changing the tonality from minor to
major and so the context of the scale, the same notes can turn a solemn,
reflective plainchant into a cheerful, lively folk song.

Verse and chorus

Often songs are split into sections, the most common sections being verses and choruses. Similar to call and response (see Lesson 16), the verses usually have different words whereas the chorus is the same every time. This song has two verses and two choruses, however, it could have as many verses as you wanted.

EXERCISE 2

Here are some other major pentatonic scales for you to practice—they are written as one octave scales but try to extend over your full range.

Accents

Most of the quarter-notes in "The Five Spot" (see opposite) are marked with an arrow head symbol. This is called an accent and means that the notes are to be played with an extra emphasis. The notes should be punchy and will help to give this piece a jazzy feel.

PRACTICE TUNE "THE FIVE SPOT" • TRACK 67

This is a swing/jazz style tune that uses major pentatonic scales.
Remember that the "swing" direction at the start of the piece means that
you should swing the eighth-notes—if in doubt look back to Lesson 10.

This piece uses letters to mark the different sections. Music is often
marked in this way because it helps to make a clear difference between
the sections. This piece has four clear sections of eight bars—the first (A)
section is repeated making two sections, the B section is the third and
the last section is the same as the first and so is labeled as another A
section. This makes the "form" of the tune "AABA." Try to be clear in your
head where you are in the form as you are playing the piece.

EXERCISE 3

Remember the recurring accidentals in the B section, in that they are only marked once in each bar. Here is the B section with all the accidentals marked. Play this again to see if you remembered to play the accidentals in "The Five Spot."

You should now be aware of the sound of the pentatonic scales. These versatile scales are capable of creating a huge range of melodies and so have been adopted by a variety of different cultures and musical genres.

TOP TUNE–POP/FUNK/SOUL
Maceo Parker "I Feel Good" with James Brown
Parker's funky alto saxophone playing is a massive part of the sound of this 1965 recording and the James Brown band in general—also listen to "Papa's Got A Brand New Bag."

Michael Brecker
March 29, 1949–January 13, 2007

The most widely imitated saxophone player since John Coltrane, Michael Brecker stretched the boundaries of the saxophone farther than any of his predecessors. His phenomenal technical ability and his use of advanced playing techniques, such as his use of the "altissimo" register (using alternative fingerings to extend the range of the instrument) and "multiphonics" (creating more than one note at a time) has raised the bar for all saxophone players. Brecker was also an early pioneer of the EWI (Electronic Wind Instrument)–a synthesizer played like a saxophone but with a huge range and a wide variety of sound options.

Brecker and other musicians of his generation were influenced by rock and rhythm and blues as much as jazz, and this is evident in Brecker's early band, Dreams, and later in The Brecker Brothers, which also included his older brother Randy on trumpet. These bands favored electric instruments (electric guitars, keyboards, and bass) rather than the acoustic instruments used in jazz previously. This bridged the gap between jazz and rock music and the style became known as "fusion."

Brecker was also a prolific session musician appearing on over 500 albums and contributing some of the most famous pop saxophone solos of all time–James Taylor, Paul Simon, Eric Clapton, and Dire Straits have all called on Brecker to add his unique touch of class to their records.

Michael Brecker's work became increasingly jazz-based later in his career and he released a series of high-octane acoustic jazz albums with other high-profile jazz musicians including Herbie Hancock and Pat Metheny before his untimely death in 2007.

Key recordings: "Don't Let Me Be Lonely Tonight" with James Taylor, 1972; *Brecker Bros.*, **1975; "Still Crazy After All These Years" with Paul Simon, 1975;** *Michael Brecker*, **1987;** *Tales From The Hudson*, **1996.**

Lesson 18 • Seventh chords and the blues

In Lesson 15 we changed triads (three-note chords) to four-note chords by adding the seventh to the standard root, third, and fifth make-up of a chord. In this lesson we are going to build on the work you did on the twelve-bar blues in Lesson 14 by adding seventh chords to the blues sequence.

Adding the seventh to the twelve-bar blues

Look back to Lesson 14 and remind yourself of the twelve-bar blues sequence and its use of the I, IV, and V chords. To make the blues sound more authentic we are going to make each of the chords a seventh by adding a flattened seventh to each.

EXERCISE 1

The color of these seventh chords is created by the clash between the major third and the flattened seventh. Practice playing the chords one note at a time to familiarize yourself with their sound.

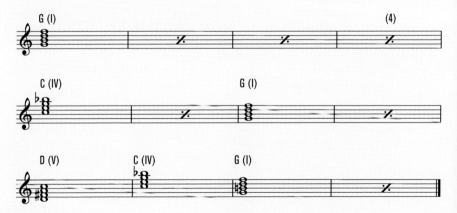

EXERCISE 2

This exercise uses the thirds and sevenths of the chords (the G7 and C7 chords also have the roots for reference). Play along with the backing track that includes four choruses (repeats) of the twelve-bar blues.

Major and minor thirds within the blues

If you compare the use of these thirds and sevenths within these chords and the blues scale we previously used (see page 99) you will see that the new notes give you more variety within the blues sequence. The biggest difference is the sound of the major third— in this case B natural. The G blues scale uses a B♭ all the way through to create the minor sound characteristic of the style, however technically, the G7 chord has a major third. By contrasting the B natural and the B flat you can create more contrasts within a blues solo.

TOP TUNE–JAZZ
Paul Desmond "Take 5"
with Dave Brubeck
From Dave Brubeck's 1959 album *Time Out*, this is probably the most famous tune ever written in the uncommon time signature of 5/4 (see page 36).

PRACTICE TUNE "GOOD TIME BLUES" • TRACK 68

Here is a blues "head" and solo on a twelve-bar blues in G. Notice the use of the B flats and naturals within the solo and the effect they create. The blues scale is combined with regular scales too.

This tune follows the format of may blues and jazz tunes—the tune or "head" is played first followed by solos, then the head is played again at the end of the tune.

Feel free to replace the head or solo with your own improvisation—the blues is a very approachable form and hopefully you will have lots of your own ideas!

Tenuto marks/Staccato

Notice the lines over some of the quarter-notes in "Good Time Blues." These are telling you to make the notes long and smooth. The dots above the notes are known as staccato and mean the notes should be short and punchy. Contrast these with the accents introduced in Lesson 17 (see page 114).

Branford Marsalis
August 26, 1960–

PLAYER PROFILE

Combining jazz, classical, and pop saxophone styles is a tall order, but Branford Marsalis has succeeded to the highest level over his career. Born into a large musical family in Louisiana, Marsalis got his first break playing for legendary drummer Art Blakey's Jazz Messengers, a seedbed of young jazz talent since the 1950s.

The Branford Marsalis Quartet formed in the mid-1990s has become one of the most celebrated small jazz groups in the world. The group has overlooked technological advances in music and focuses entirely on intricate, acoustic jazz at the highest level of solo and ensemble performance.

In 2001 Branford Marsalis released *Creation*, an album of classical saxophone music with the Orpheus Chamber Orchestra in which he tackles classical repertoire by composers Darius Milhaud and Jacques Ibert.

Marsalis' pop work was initially centered on his jazz/hip-hop outfit Buckshot LeFonque—in contrast to his acoustic jazz work, the group featured DJs and rappers, in a dynamic blend of styles. Marsalis has also worked as a session player contributing beautiful solos to many pop records, most famously the soprano saxophone solo on Sting's "Englishman In New York."

Key recordings: *Buckshot LeFonque*, 1994; *Creation* with Orpheus Chamber Orchestra, 2001; *Metamorphosen* with Branford Marsalis Quartet, 2009.

Lesson 19 • The low register

So far you have only played notes as low as D. This
lesson will introduce you to the lowest four notes on the
saxophone and build your fluency in the lower register.

**Fingering
for low C**
Playing the
low notes on
the saxophone
involves both
your little fingers.
To play a low C, finger
a low D and add your
right little finger to the
lower of the two keys.

EXERCISE 1 • TRACK 69

Practice moving from low D to C by playing the following exercises. Try to
move smoothly between the notes—you will need lots of air and strong
support from your diaphragm. To start with, play all these exercises
forte—aim for a big, resonant sound.

Fingering for low A♯/B♭

The lowest note on the saxophone is B♭. To play this you need to add your left little finger to the low C fingering—the left little finger operates the four keys by your left hand. The B♭ key is the lowest of the four keys.

EXERCISE 2 · TRACK 70

Practice the following exercises to add low B♭ to your repertoire.

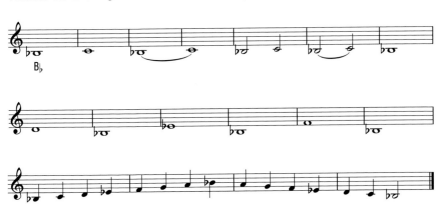

TOP TUNE–POP/FUNK/SOUL
Wilton Felder "Streetlife" with The Jazz Crusaders
Felder's famous solo on this 1979 Jazz Crusaders' classic is a great slice of top-class jazz/funk saxophone playing.

Fingering for low B natural and C#/D♭

The two middle little finger keys are used for B natural and C#.
The inside key is for B and the outside is C#.

EXERCISE 3 · TRACK 71

Practice the following exercises to add low B natural and C# to your repertoire.

The chromatic scale

The chromatic scale is one that is built entirely of semitones.
This makes it neither major nor minor. Chromatic scales are
used to decorate melodies and add "passing" notes between
the stronger notes of a key. Because a chromatic scale uses
every available note, all the scales are the same—only the
starting note differs.

EXERCISE 4 · TRACK 72

Here is a chromatic scale starting on low D and going
down to low B♭—this is a great exercise to practice your
low notes. Play this slowly at first and gradually increase
the tempo as your little finger moves more freely.

EXERCISE 5 · TRACK 73

Here is a one-octave chromatic scale from low C. There
are 12 notes in a one-octave chromatic scale rather than
the eight in a standard major or minor scale.

EXERCISE 6 · TRACK 74

This piece sets up a funky bass-line-style groove. This
sort of line is often played on a baritone saxophone (an
octave lower than the alto sax) and is a feature of soul
and Motown music.

Playing in the low register takes a lot of trial and error—
don't worry if at first it sounds a little raucous and honky.
The more time you spend down there the easier it gets.
Your little fingers might ache after a while too, so take
care not to overstrain them. Practicing a little and often is
the answer.

Lesson 20 • The high register

In this lesson you will learn the highest five notes on the saxophone. This will mean that you've covered the whole range of the instrument from low B♭ to high F♯. To play the higher notes will involve you using the "palm keys" at the top of the instrument. These are played with the inside of your left hand.

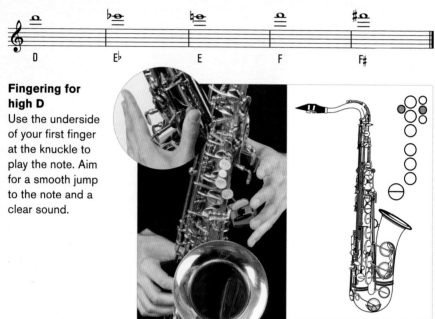

Fingering for high D
Use the underside of your first finger at the knuckle to play the note. Aim for a smooth jump to the note and a clear sound.

EXERCISE 1
Play the below exercises to build fluency for high D.

EXERCISE 1 A • TRACK 75

EXERCISE 1 B • TRACK 75

Check the ledger lines

High D looks a bit like a high B in that it is written above the stave and above a ledger line. D, however, is written above a second ledger line—be sure to check the number of ledger lines for the higher notes.

Fingering for high D♯/E♭
To play high E♭ add the second palm key as demonstrated. Be sure to hold down the D key as well.

EXERCISE 2
Play these exercises to build fluency for high E♭.

EXERCISE 2A · TRACK 76

EXERCISE 2B · TRACK 76

Exercise 2b will take some practice—the jumps up to the E♭ will feel difficult at first. Practice slowly and make sure the jumps are smooth. Note that E♭ is the same note as D♯. In this exercise they are written as E♭.

Fingering for high E

High E uses the same two palm keys as the E♭ but adds one of the side keys operated with the inside knuckle of your right hand.

EXERCISE 3

Practice these exercises for high E. Note that in this exercise E♭ is written as D♯.

EXERCISE 3A • TRACK 77

EXERCISE 3B • TRACK 77

Fingering for high F

To play high F, add the third left-hand palm key to the high E fingering. The combination of all three palm keys and the right-hand side key feels a little awkward at first but the fingering combinations will get easier with practice.

EXERCISE 4

Practice the following exercises for high F.

EXERCISE 4A • TRACK 78

EXERCISE 4B • TRACK 78

Fingering for high F♯/G♭

Most modern saxophones have a high F♯ key operated with your right-hand third finger. Traditionally the upper range of the saxophone was high F but the F♯ was added later. None of the pieces in this book use high F♯ but the Complete fingering charts (see pages 140–155) and Scale library (see pages 156–211) include F♯ in case you encounter it in any other pieces you play.

EXERCISE 5 · TRACK 79

This chromatic scale will help you learn the fingerings and sounds of all the high-register notes on the saxophone.

PRACTICE TUNE "FLYING HIGH" • TRACK 80

This piece will help you to navigate the high register. It contains all of the new notes introduced in this chapter (except high F#).

Andante

Italian terms

In the early days of music notation Italian was the standard language. You are hopefully comfortable using the Italian terms for the dynamics of music: *forte*, *piano*, mezzo piano etc. Italian terms are also used to explain the tempo and mood of a piece. There is a list of Italian terms on page 248. The *andante* instruction at the start of this means to play "at a walking pace." This is of course open to interpretation but is a useful guide to the tempo.

TOP TUNE–POP/ FUNK/SOUL
Candy Dulfer
"Lily Was Here"
with Dave Stewart
Dutch saxophonist Candy Dulfer's 1990 hit with Dave Stewart showcases her smooth jazz style.

Lesson 21 • Jazz

Jazz is the style of music most associated with the saxophone. Since it started to be used in the 1920s, the saxophone and jazz have gone hand in hand as successive generations of musical pioneers have made the instrument their own.

The history of jazz

Jazz music initially grew up in the bars and clubs of New Orleans in the early part of the twentieth century. New Orleans was a thriving and diverse port city and had a huge turnover of different peoples and their cultures. The military music of the army and navy bases mixed with the blues music of the American South and the songs and rhythms of the African population entering New Orleans. The resulting music was a rich harmonic and rhythmic blend of the different elements. The early jazz styles from New Orleans are called "dixie," "ragtime," or "New Orleans jazz," and are often grouped together under the title "traditional jazz." Perhaps the most famous exponent of traditional (often abbreviated to "trad.") jazz is Louis Armstrong. Armstrong was a trumpet virtuoso and singer whose distinct style on both the trumpet and vocals made him a legendary performer and American icon.

The saxophone wasn't really used in jazz at this time—the clarinet was the preferred woodwind instrument, possibly because of its use in the military bands. See pages 10–17 for more on the history of the saxophone and its establishment in different musical styles.

The great jazz sax players

There are many resources available to discover the great jazz saxophone players. A rough chronological journey should include Sidney Bechet, Coleman Hawkins, Lester Young, Johnny Hodges, Charlie Parker, Sonny Rollins, and John Coltrane. This is by no means an exhaustive guide but these players have made huge advances in both music and saxophone playing and should be listened to by anyone interested in jazz. See the player profiles in the lessons for information on other important jazz saxophone players.

Bebop boys
From left to right: Charlie Parker, Dizzy
Gillespie, and a young John Coltrane.

Norwegian woodwind
Jan Garbarek playing the tenor saxophone in concert in Hamburg, Germany.

Improvisation

Jazz is famous for improvisation: spontaneous composition. Jazz musicians often play the melody of the piece and then repeat the structure and replace the melody with their own tune. Originally the improvisations were just repeats of the melody with a few additional embellishments, but as the music has developed so too have the improvisations. Modern jazz improvisation is an incredibly subtle and intricate art form born out of these early variations on a theme.

Jazz form: head and solo

In a jazz performance the "head" or melody is played at the start of the piece. This sets the tone and style of the piece for the improvisation that follows. In "Storyville Stomp" (on the following pages) the head is marked (A and B) and is over the first 32 bars of the piece. After the head, the improvisation starts. This is played over the existing form of the piece, and the band will play A and B as before but this time with an improvised variation or "solo." Each repeat of the A and B sequence is called a "chorus."

The recorded version of "Storyville Stomp" has three choruses in total. This allows for:

Head—A and B (32 bars)
Solo—A and B (32 bars)
Head—A and B (32 bars)

Note that the head is usually played at the end too to round off the performance.

PRACTICE TUNE "STORYVILLE STOMP" • TRACK 81

This is a raucous trad-style Dixie tune named after the notorious
Storyville district of New Orleans. The tune has two sections of 16 bars
(A and B). The entire form of the tune is 32 bars. A written solo has been
included on pages 138–139—this continues where the head leaves off
and will enable you to play in a New Orleans style from the beginning.

When you have mastered the written solo, try to play your own solo
over the chords. The notes for each chord are included in the lower
stave—these tell you what notes the rhythm section are playing and will
be important for your improvisations because you will need to know
which notes sound good over which chords. The rhythm and style are
up to you!

Note that the notes (root, third, fifth, and seventh) of each chord have
been given, although in most music, only the chord symbol is given.

TOP TUNE–CLASSICAL/CONTEMPORARY
Darius Milhaud "Scaramouche"
This work for alto saxophone and orchestra from
1937 is an important work for contemporary
saxophone players.

2 Complete Fingering Charts

Each new note is introduced and explained in the lessons section of the book. However, if you need to quickly check a fingering then this section will help you identify it easily. All the notes are featured, accompanied by diagrams and photographs for an at-a-glance reference. The red spots on the saxophone diagrams mean that your fingers are to be pressed down.

Fingering charts at a glance

B	A	G	C	F	E

D	B	A	G	C	F

E	D	F#/G♭	F#/G♭	A#/B♭

A♯/B♭	D♯/E♭	D♯/E♭	C♯/D♭	C♯/D♭
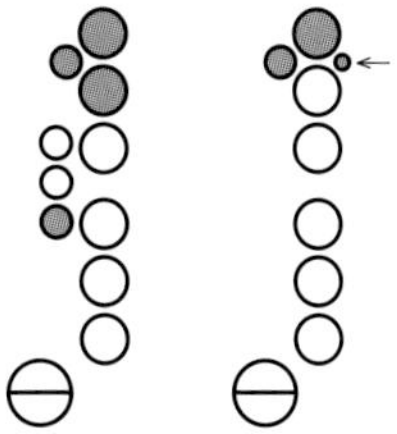	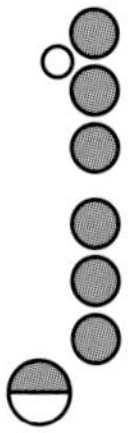	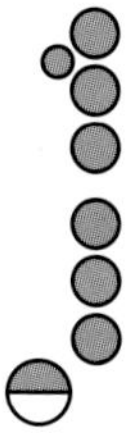	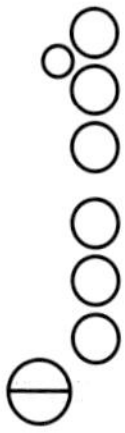	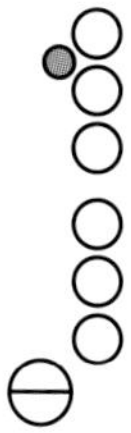

G♯/A♭	G♯/A♭	C	A♯/B♭	B	C♯/D♭
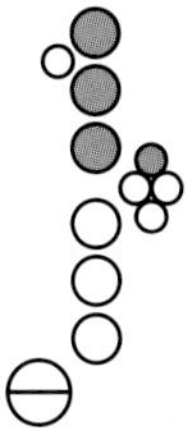	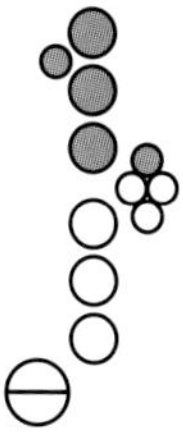	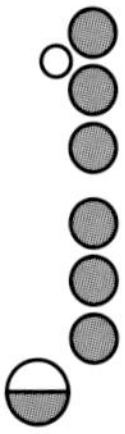	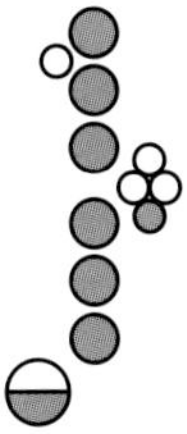	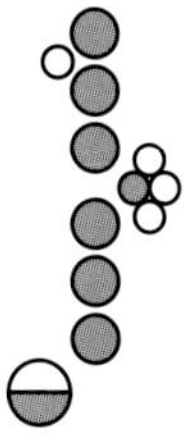	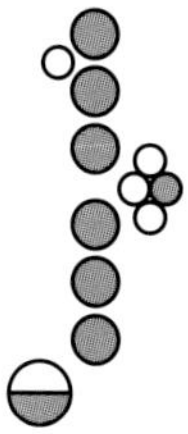

D	D♯/E♭	E	F	F♯
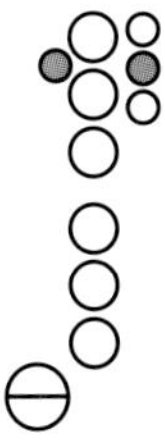	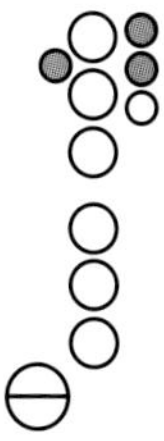	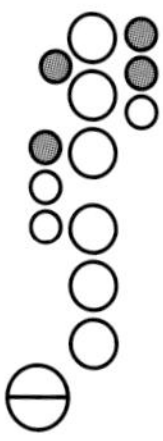	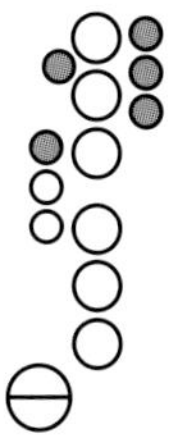	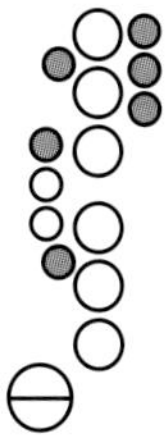

B

A

G

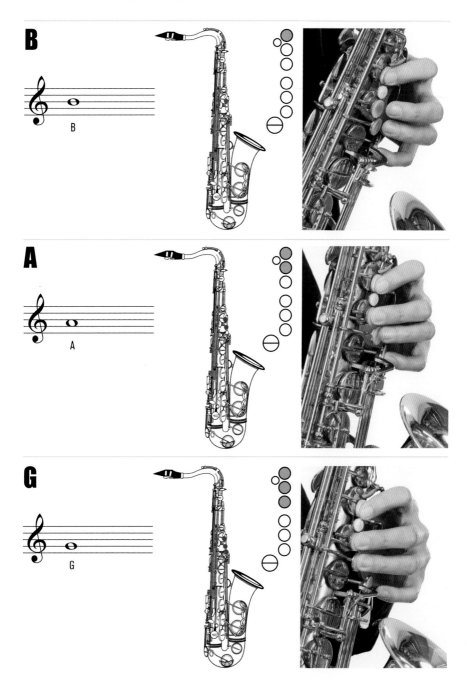

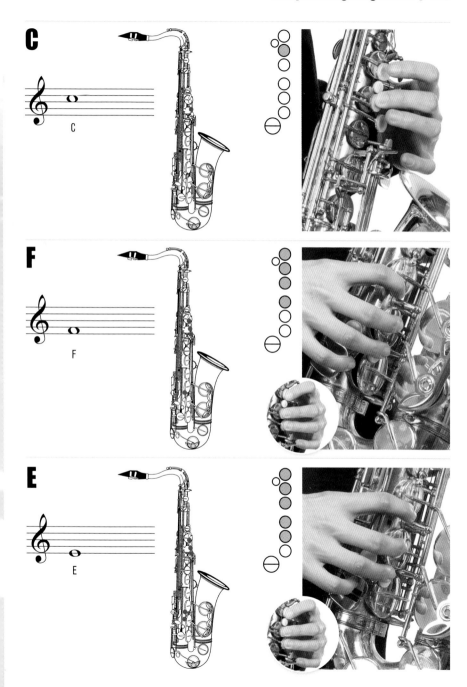

C

C

F

F

E

E

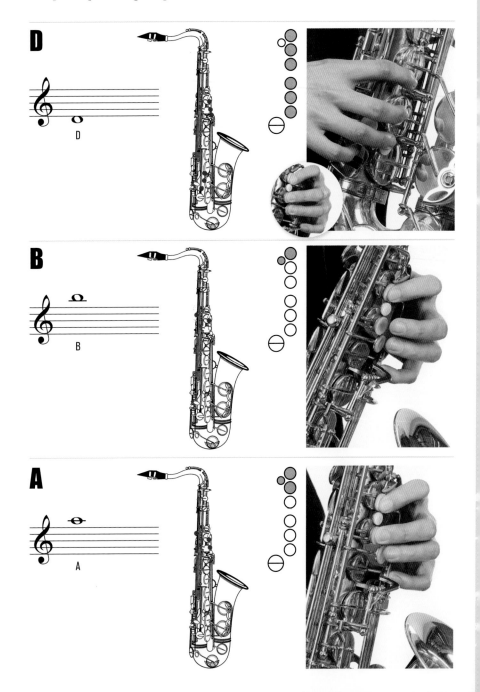

D

D

B

B

A

A

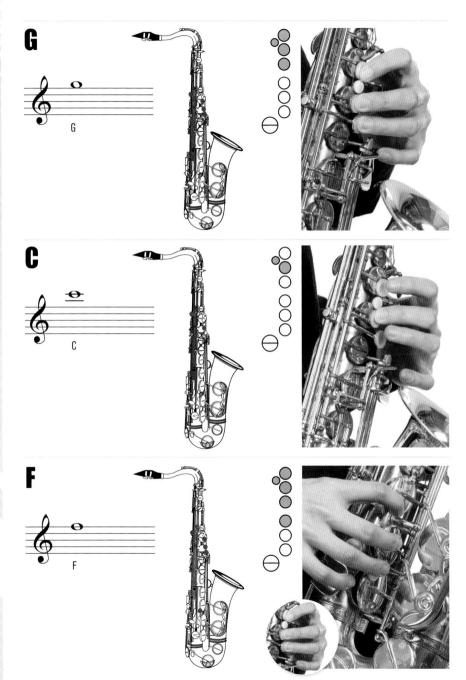

G

G

C

C

F

F

E

D

F♯/G♭

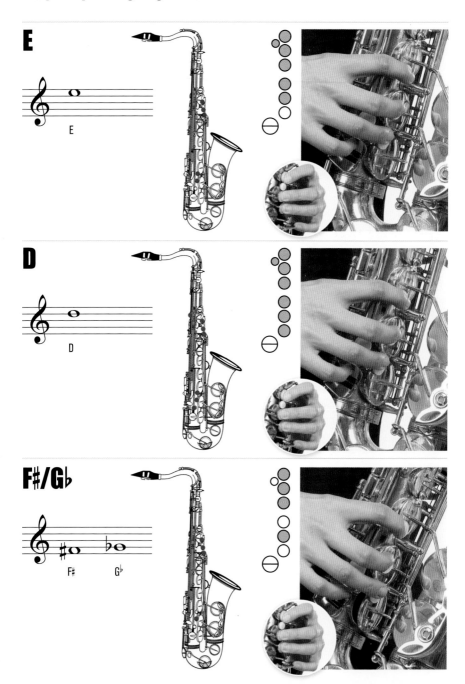

F#/Gb

F#   Gb

A#/Bb
Side fingering

A#   Bb

A#/Bb
Button fingering

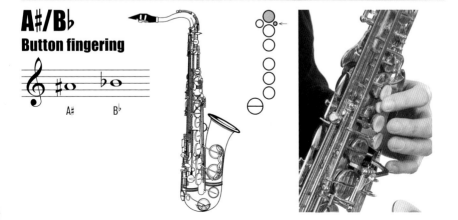

A#   Bb

A#/B♭
Side fingering

A#   B♭

A#/B♭
Button fingering

A#   B♭

D#/E♭

D#   E♭

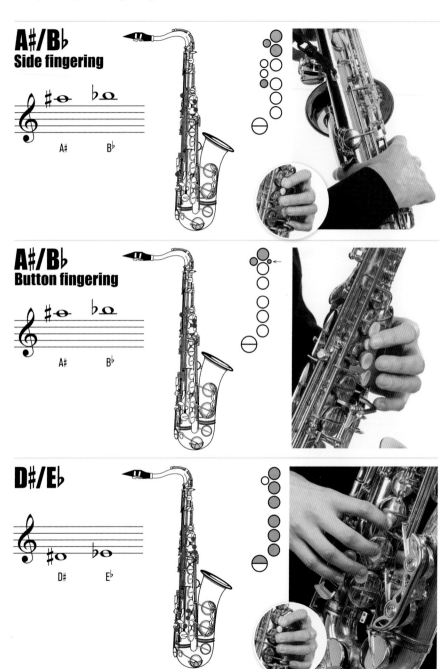

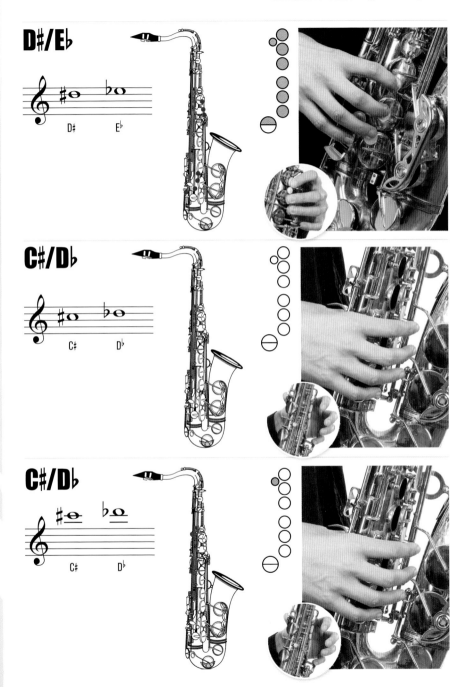

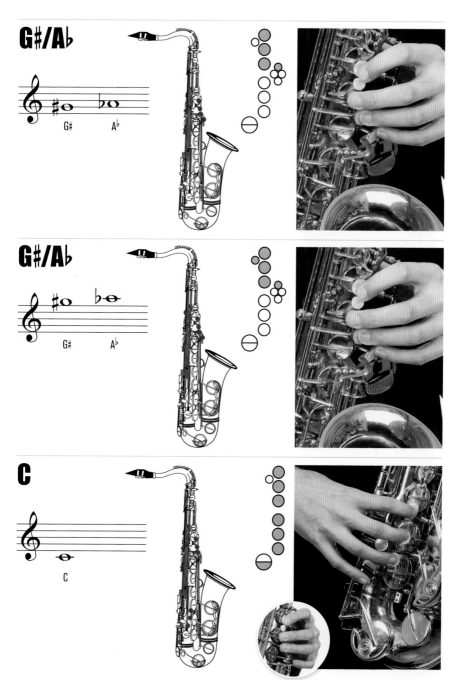

A♯/B♭

A♯   B♭

B

B

C♯/D♭

C♯   D♭

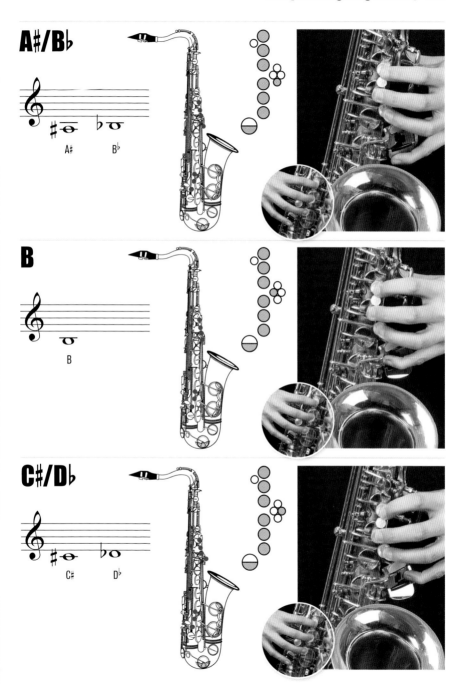

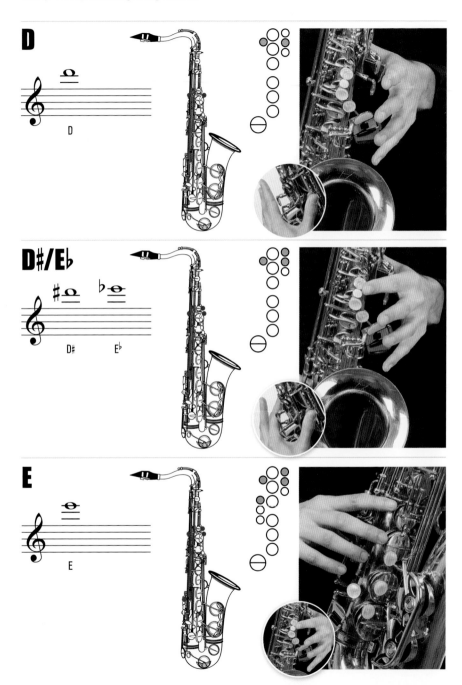

D

D

D♯/E♭

D♯ E♭

E

E

F

F

F#

F#

3 Scale Library

The scale library contains all of the different scales introduced throughout the lessons. All are grouped together by key, starting with the major scale and including the melodic and harmonic minors, Dorian and Mixolydian modes, and the blues scale and twelve-bar blues chord sequence, as well as arpeggios and chord voicings for all the above. These scales form the basic scale repertoire in classical music as well as some of the scales used for jazz and improvised music.

Scale library introduction

In the scale library, all the scales you will need to improve both your saxophone technique and your general musicality and understanding are shown in full.

Scale library organization

For each key, eight of the most common scales for that key are featured together with arpeggios and chords. The major and minor scales are covered as well as pentatonics and the two most common modes–Mixolydian and Dorian. There are also chord voicings for minor 7 and seventh chords as well as a twelve-bar blues in each key.

Chord voicings

Chapter 15 introduced you to four-note chords comprised of the root, third, fifth, and seventh. The various combinations of thirds and sevenths create a variety of chord types and the most common ones are written here for your convenience. The symbol m7 is used for a minor seventh chord while just a 7 after the letter name means a seventh chord.

Modes

The modes are an alternative set of scales derived from the major scale. The modes have been used for centuries and each has a Greek name. They can be used to improvise over different types of chords–the "Dorian" mode fits well over a minor seventh chord and the "Mixolydian" mode contains the notes of the seventh chord.

Twelve-bar blues

Chapter 18 introduced you to the twelve-bar blues. This is possibly the most common chord sequence used in jazz/rock (and of course blues) music. The blues isn't always played in one key, and if you are playing in bands it's useful to know the twelve-bar blues in various keys. The scale library includes a standard twelve-bar blues for each key.

Enharmonic notes

As you are aware, a sharp note has an equivalent flat and vice versa–F♯ is the same note as G♭, E♭ the same as D♯ etc. (see Lesson 7). Notes that sound the same but with different flat/sharp names are called "enharmonic equivalents" of each other. In keys with only a few sharps or flats it is easy to decide whether to call a note a sharp or its enharmonic equivalent flat: in G major for example, the F needs to be sharpened to F♯; this note could technically be written as a G♭ however, the F♯'s purpose is as a replacement F.

In keys with lots of sharps and flats it is often easier to write the major key with flats and the minor key with sharps. D♭ minor is a very complicated key to navigate and so is seldom used–it is much easier to read as C♯ minor, and for

C major (A minor)

F major (D minor)

G major (E minor)

B♭ major (G minor)

D major (B minor)

E♭ major (C minor)

Circle of fifths

A major (F♯ minor)

A♭ major (F minor)

E major (C♯ minor)

D♭ major (B♭ minor)

B major (G♯ minor)

G♭ major (E♭ minor)

F♯ major (D♯ minor)

Circle of fifths
The Scale library is organized by a musical principle called the circle of fifths (see page 241).

this reason the minor scales, arpeggios, m7 chord voicing, and pentatonic scales are written as C♯ minor in the Scale library.

The same difficulties occur in A♭ minor (written here as G♯ minor) and G♭ minor (written here as F♯ minor.)

You will notice that G♭ and F♯ sound the same, since they are the same notes with different names. Two versions of this scale are featured—G♭ major with six flats and F♯ major with six sharps (see above). When playing the more complicated keys, remember that all the sharps and flats are there to preserve the tone/semitone pattern from which the major scale is constructed (see Lesson 8). Try to use your ear when playing these scales and you will quickly hear which notes are right and wrong.

Practicing scales

Practicing scales should be a part of your practice routine, and is a great way of improving your technique, especially in terms of developing finger strength and speed. Because scales are less creatively demanding, you can focus more on technical matters such as transition between notes and hand position. Aim for an even tone, practice at different tempos (although never try to play them faster than you can control), and use different articulations from a short and sharp *staccato* to a smooth, lyrical *legato*. Each will develop a different area of your technique and help you to become better saxophonist.

C scale library

Major scale

Major arpeggio

Harmonic minor scale

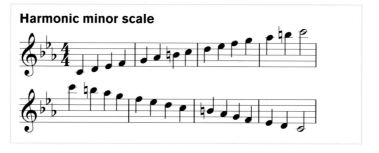

Harmonic minor scale

Below is the harmonic minor with the major key signature plus accidentals, to show how the minor scale is derived from the major (see Lesson 11).

C

F

B♭

E♭

A♭ /
G♯

D♭ /
C♯

G♭

G

D

A

E

B

F♯

C

F

B♭

E♭

A♭ / G#

D♭ / C#

G♭

G

D

A

E

B

F♯

Melodic minor scale

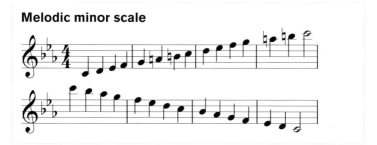

Melodic minor scale

Below is the melodic minor with the major key signature plus accidentals, to show how the minor scale is derived from the major (see Lesson 11).

Minor arpeggio

Mixolydian scale

C
F
B♭
E♭
A♭ / G#
D♭ / C#
G♭
G
D
A
E
B
F#

Seventh chord voicing

Dorian scale

Minor seventh chord voicing

Major pentatonic scale

Minor pentatonic scale

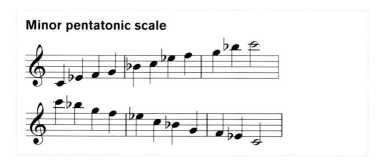

Blues scale

Twelve-bar blues

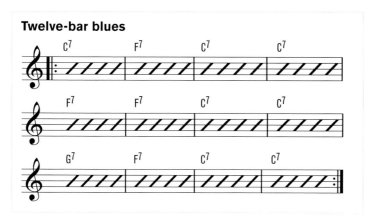

C

F

B♭

E♭

A♭ / G♯

D♭ / C♯

G♭

G

D

A

E

B

F♯

F scale library

C

F

B♭

E♭

A♭ /
G♯

D♭ /
C♯

G♭

G

D

A

E

B

F♯

Major scale

Major arpeggio

Harmonic minor scale

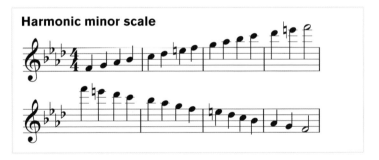

Harmonic minor scale

Below is the harmonic minor with the major key signature plus accidentals, to show how the minor scale is derived from the major (see Lesson 11).

C

F

B♭

E♭

A♭ /
G♯

D♭ /
C♯

G♭

G

D

A

E

B

F♯

Melodic minor scale

Melodic minor scale

Below is the melodic minor with the major key signature plus accidentals, to show how the minor scale is derived from the major (see Lesson 11).

Minor arpeggio

Mixolydian scale

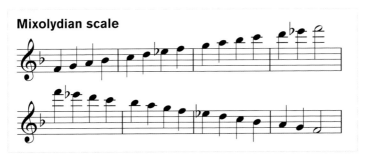

Seventh chord voicing

Dorian scale

Minor seventh chord voicing

Major pentatonic scale

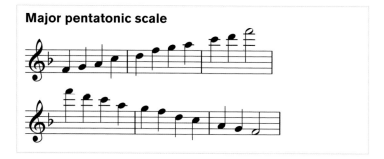

C

F

B♭

E♭

A♭ /
G♯

D♭ /
C♯

G♭

G

D

A

E

B

F♯

Minor pentatonic scale

Blues scale

Twelve-bar blues

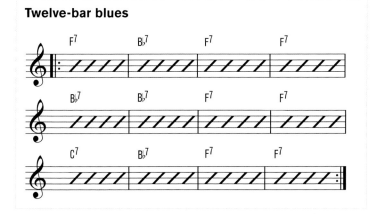

B♭ scale library

Major scale

Major arpeggio

Harmonic minor scale

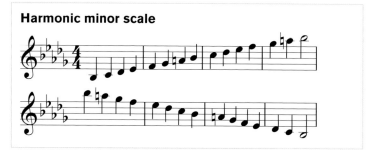

Harmonic minor scale

Below is the harmonic minor with the major key signature plus accidentals, to show how the minor scale is derived from the major (see Lesson 11).

C

F

B♭

E♭

A♭ / G♯

D♭ / C♯

G♭

G

D

A

E

B

F♯

C

F

B♭

E♭

A♭ /
G♯

D♭ /
C♯

G♭

G

D

A

E

B

F♯

Melodic minor scale

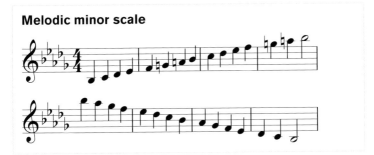

Melodic minor scale

Below is the melodic minor with the major key signature plus accidentals, to show how the minor scale is derived from the major (see Lesson 11).

Minor arpeggio

Mixolydian scale

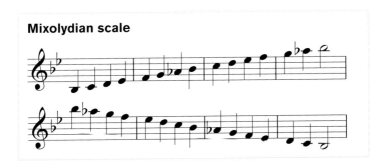

C
F
B♭
E♭
A♭ / G♯
D♭ / C♯
G♭
G
D
A
E
B
F♯

Seventh chord voicing

Dorian scale

Minor seventh chord voicing

Major pentatonic scale

C

F

B♭

E♭

A♭ /
G#

D♭ /
C#

G♭

G

D

A

E

B

F#

Minor pentatonic scale

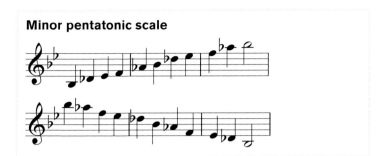

Blues scale

Twelve-bar blues

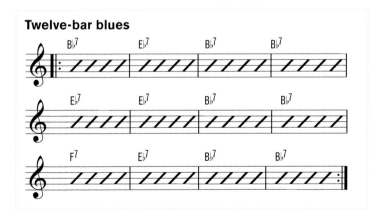

E♭ scale library

Major scale

Major arpeggio

Harmonic minor scale

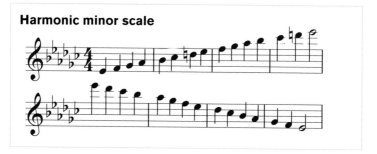

Harmonic minor scale

Below is the harmonic minor with the major key signature plus accidentals, to show how the minor scale is derived from the major (see Lesson 11).

C

F

B♭

E♭

A♭ / G♯

D♭ / C♯

G♭

G

D

A

E

B

F♯

C

F

Bb

Eb

Ab /
G#

Db /
C#

Gb

G

D

A

E

B

F#

Melodic minor scale

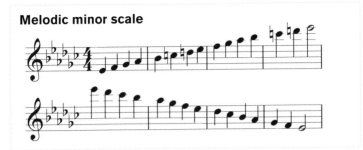

Melodic minor scale

Below is the melodic minor with the major key signature plus accidentals, to show how the minor scale is derived from the major (see Lesson 11).

Minor arpeggio

Mixolydian scale

Seventh chord voicing

Dorian scale

Minor seventh chord voicing

Major pentatonic scale

Minor pentatonic scale

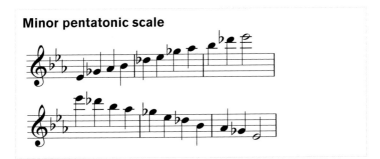

Blues scale

Twelve-bar blues

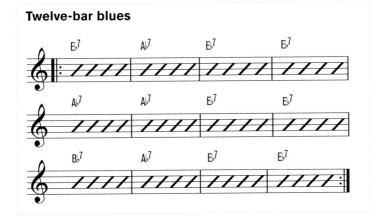

C

F

B♭

E♭

A♭ / G#

D♭ / C#

G♭

G

D

A

E

B

F#

C

F

B♭

E♭

A♭ / G♯

D♭ / C♯

G♭

G

D

A

E

B

F♯

A♭ /G♯ scale library

Major scale

Major arpeggio

Harmonic minor scale

A♭ harmonic minor is notated as its enharmonic, G♯ minor. In this format, the scale is easier to read, play, and understand.

Melodic minor scale

A♭ melodic minor is notated as its enharmonic, G♯ minor. In this format, the scale is easier to read, play, and understand.

Minor arpeggio

A♭ minor arpeggio is notated as its enharmonic, G♯ minor. In this format, the arpeggio is easier to read, play, and understand.

Mixolydian scale

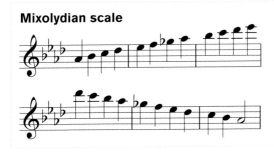

C

F

B♭

E♭

A♭ / G♯

D♭ / C♯

G♭

G

D

A

E

B

F♯

Seventh chord voicing

Dorian scale

Minor seventh chord voicing

A♭ minor seventh chord voicing is notated as its enharmonic, G♯. In this format, the chord voicing is easier to read, play, and understand.

Major pentatonic scale

C

F

Bb

Eb

Ab /
G#

Db /
C#

Gb

G

D

A

E

B

F#

Minor pentatonic scale

Ab minor pentatonic is notated as its enharmonic, G# minor pentatonic. In this format, the scale is easier to read, play, and understand.

Blues scale

Twelve-bar blues

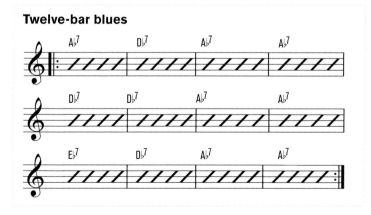

D♭/C♯ scale library

Major scale

Major arpeggio

Harmonic minor scale

D♭ harmonic minor is notated as its enharmonic, C♯ minor. In this format, the scale is easier to read, play, and understand.

C
F
B♭
E♭
A♭ / G♯
D♭ / C♯
G♭
G
D
A
E
B
F♯

C

F

B♭

E♭

A♭ /
G♯

D♭ /
C♯

G♭

G

D

A

E

B

F♯

Melodic minor scale

D♭ melodic minor is notated as its enharmonic, C♯ minor. In this format, the scale is easier to read, play, and understand.

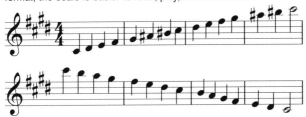

Minor arpeggio

D♭ minor arpeggio is notated as its enharmonic, C♯ minor. In this format, the arpeggio is easier to read, play, and understand.

Mixolydian scale

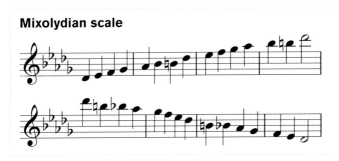

C
F
B♭
E♭
A♭ /
G#
D♭ /
C#
G♭
G
D
A
E
B
F#

Seventh chord voicing

Dorian scale

Minor seventh chord voicing

D♭ minor seventh chord voicing is notated as its enharmonic, C#. In this format, the chord voicing is easier to read, play, and understand.

Major pentatonic scale

Minor pentatonic scale

Db minor pentatonic is notated as its enharmonic, C# minor pentatonic. In this format, the scale is easier to read, play, and understand.

Blues scale

Twelve-bar blues

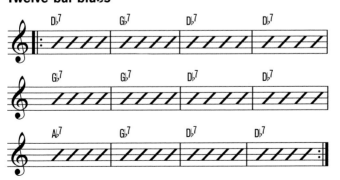

G♭ scale library

Major scale

Major arpeggio

Minor scales

G♭ harmonic and melodic minors are notated as the enharmonic, F♯ minor (see pages 208–211). In this format, the scales are easier to read, play, and understand. On these pages you will also find F♯ minor arpeggio, minor seventh chord voicing, and minor pentatonic scale.

Mixolydian scale

C

F

B♭

E♭

A♭ / G♯

D♭ / C♯

G♭

G

D

A

E

B

F♯

C

F

B♭

E♭

A♭ /
G♯

D♭ /
C♯

G♭

G

D

A

E

B

F♯

Seventh chord voicing

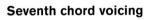

Dorian scale

Major pentatonic scale

C

F

B♭

E♭

A♭ /
G#

D♭ /
C#

G♭

G

D

A

E

B

F#

Blues scale

Twelve-bar blues

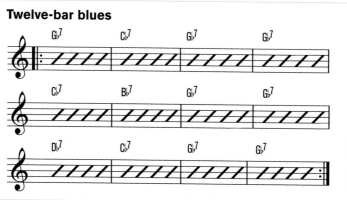

G♭ major
G♭ major can be tricky to play—try using the side B♭ fingering (see page 52) for a smooth movement between B♭ and B natural.

G scale library

Major scale

Major arpeggio

Harmonic minor scale

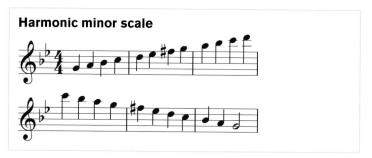

Harmonic minor scale

Below is the harmonic minor with the major key signature plus accidentals, to show how the minor scale is derived from the major (see Lesson 11).

C

F

B♭

E♭

A♭ / G♯

D♭ / C♯

G♭

G

D

A

E

B

F♯

C

F

B♭

E♭

A♭ /
G♯

D♭ /
C♯

G♭

G

D

A

E

B

F♯

Melodic minor scale

Melodic minor scale

Below is the melodic minor with the major key signature plus accidentals, to show how the minor scale is derived from the major (see Lesson 11).

Minor arpeggio

Mixolydian scale

C

F

B♭

E♭

A♭ /
G#

D♭ /
C#

G♭

G

D

A

E

B

F#

Seventh chord voicing

Dorian scale

Minor seventh chord voicing

Major pentatonic scale

Minor pentatonic scale

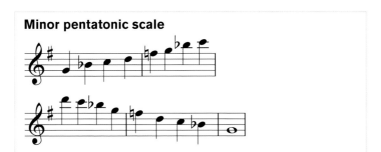

Blues scale

Twelve-bar blues

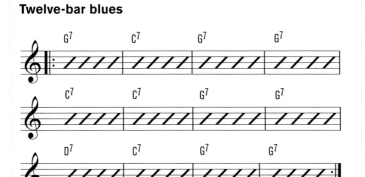

C

F

B♭

E♭

A♭ / G♯

D♭ / C♯

G♭

G

D

A

E

B

F♯

D scale library

Major scale

Major arpeggio

Harmonic minor scale

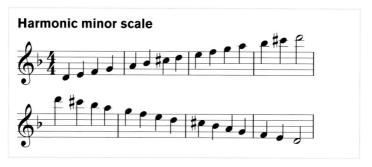

Harmonic minor scale

Below is the harmonic minor with the major key signature plus accidentals, to show how the minor scale is derived from the major (see Lesson 11).

C

F

B♭

E♭

A♭ / G#

D♭ / C#

G♭

G

D

A

E

B

F#

C

F

B♭

E♭

A♭ /
G♯

D♭ /
C♯

G♭

G

D

A

E

B

F♯

Melodic minor scale

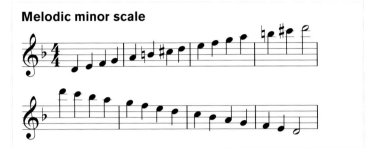

Melodic minor scale

Below is the melodic minor with the major key signature plus accidentals, to show how the minor scale is derived from the major (see Lesson 11).

Minor arpeggio

Mixolydian scale

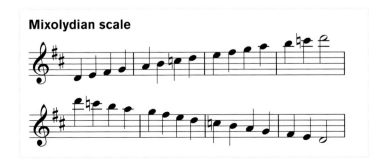

Seventh chord voicing

Dorian scale

Minor seventh chord voicing

Major pentatonic scale

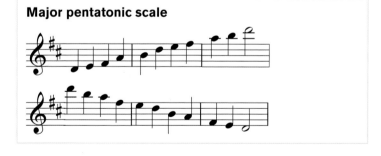

Minor pentatonic scale

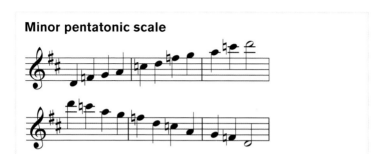

Blues scale

Twelve-bar blues

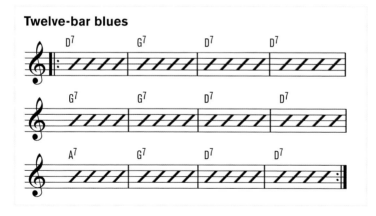

C

F

B♭

E♭

A♭ /
G♯

D♭ /
C♯

G♭

G

D

A

E

B

F♯

A scale library

Major scale

Major arpeggio

Harmonic minor scale

Harmonic minor scale

Below is the harmonic minor with the major key signature plus accidentals, to show how the minor scale is derived from the major (see Lesson 11).

C

F

B♭

E♭

A♭ /
G♯

D♭ /
C♯

G♭

G

D

A

E

B

F♯

Melodic minor scale

Melodic minor scale

Below is the melodic minor with the major key signature plus accidentals, to show how the minor scale is derived from the major (see Lesson 11).

Minor arpeggio

Mixolydian scale

Seventh chord voicing

Dorian scale

Minor seventh chord voicing

Major pentatonic scale

Minor pentatonic scale

Blues scale

Twelve-bar blues

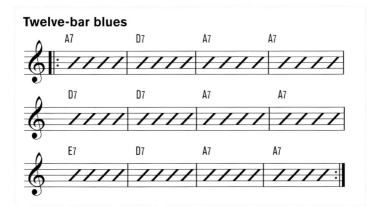

C

F

B♭

E♭

A♭ /
G♯

D♭ /
C♯

G♭

G

D

A

E

B

F♯

E scale library

Major scale

Major arpeggio

Harmonic minor scale

Harmonic minor scale

Below is the harmonic minor with the major key signature plus accidentals, to show how the minor scale is derived from the major (see Lesson 11).

C
F
B♭
E♭
A♭ / G♯
D♭ / C♯
G♭
G
D
A
E
B
F♯

C

F

B♭

E♭

A♭ /
G♯

D♭ /
C♯

G♭

G

D

A

E

B

F♯

Melodic minor scale

Melodic minor scale

Below is the melodic minor with the major key signature plus accidentals, to show how the minor scale is derived from the major (see Lesson 11).

Minor arpeggio

Mixolydian scale

Seventh chord voicing

Dorian scale

Minor seventh chord voicing

Major pentatonic scale

C
F
B♭
E♭
A♭ / G#
D♭ / C#
G♭
G
D
A
E
B
F#

Minor pentatonic scale

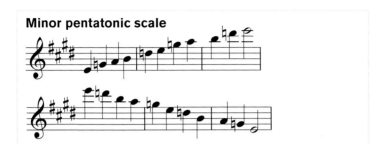

Blues scale

Twelve-bar blues

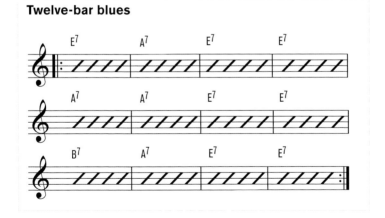

C

F

B♭

E♭

A♭ / G#

D♭ / C#

G♭

G

D

A

E

B

F#

B scale library

Major scale

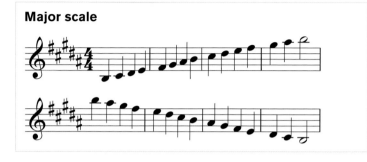

Major arpeggio

Harmonic minor scale

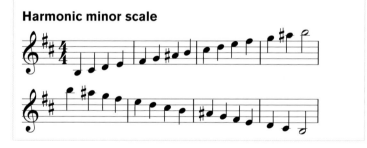

Harmonic minor scale

Below is the harmonic minor with the major key signature plus accidentals, to show how the minor scale is derived from the major (see Lesson 11).

C

F

B♭

E♭

A♭ / G♯

D♭ / C♯

G♭

G

D

A

E

B

F♯

C

F

B♭

E♭

A♭ /
G#

D♭ /
C#

G♭

G

D

A

E

B

F#

Melodic minor scale

Melodic minor scale

Below is the melodic minor with the major key signature plus accidentals, to show how the minor scale is derived from the major (see Lesson 11).

Minor arpeggio

Mixolydian scale

Seventh chord voicing

Dorian scale

Minor seventh chord voicing

Major pentatonic scale

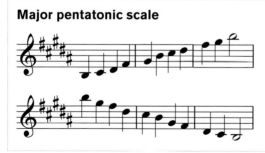

C

F

B♭

E♭

A♭ / G♯

D♭ / C♯

G♭

G

D

A

E

B

F♯

Minor pentatonic scale

Blues scale

Twelve-bar blues

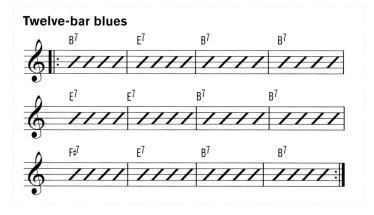

F♯ scale library

Major scale

Major arpeggio

Harmonic minor scale

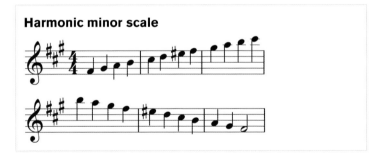

Harmonic minor scale

Below is the harmonic minor with the major key signature plus accidentals, to show how the minor scale is derived from the major (see Lesson 11).

C

F

B♭

E♭

A♭ / G♯

D♭ / C♯

G♭

G

D

A

E

B

F♯

C

F

B♭

E♭

A♭ / G♯

D♭ / C♯

G♭

G

D

A

E

B

F♯

Melodic minor scale

Melodic minor scale

Below is the melodic minor with the major key signature plus accidentals, to show how the minor scale is derived from the major (see Lesson 11).

Minor arpeggio

Mixolydian scale

C

F

B♭

E♭

A♭ /
G#

D♭ /
C#

G♭

G

D

A

E

B

F#

Seventh chord voicing

Dorian scale

Minor seventh chord voicing

Major pentatonic scale

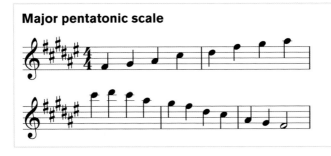

C

F

B♭

E♭

A♭ /
G#

D♭ /
C#

G♭

G

D

A

E

B

F#

Minor pentatonic scale

Blues scale

Twelve-bar blues

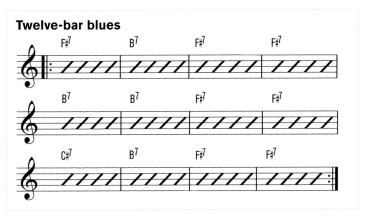

4 Practical Advice

This section of the book will help you to deal with some of the nonmusical aspects of your saxophone. The different types of saxophone are covered, as well as some tips on reeds, mouthpieces, and general care and maintenance of your instrument.

Types of saxophone

There are four main types of saxophone: soprano, alto, tenor, and baritone. They vary in size and pitch with the soprano being the smallest and highest in pitch while the baritone is the biggest and lowest in pitch. There is also a sopranino sax that is even higher than the soprano, and a bass and contrabass that have an extremely low range; however, these three are rare and not used all that often.

Transposition

The good news for us saxophone players is that the fingerings on all saxophones are the same—a written G on a soprano is the same as on a baritone or alto or tenor. This obviously makes moving between the different types of saxophone much easier. The reason that this works is because the saxophone is a "transposing" instrument. To keep the notes within the convenient low Bb to high F# range we've become used to, the lower saxes in particular have their notes written higher than they actually sound. The written and sounding (concert) ranges for each saxophone will be shown as they are introduced.

Most of the music you play (including all the material in this book) has the transposition taken into account so just play the notes written as you see them. It's really only if you are composing or conversing with other musicians that you need to be aware of the transposition.

Soprano saxophone

The soprano is the only non-curved member of the saxophone family and looks a little like a gold clarinet. (Some companies do now make a curved model that looks like a tiny alto sax.)

The soprano can be hard to play at first but once you find your voice it can be hugely rewarding to play—listen to John

Coltrane's landmark recording of "My Favorite Things" from 1961 to hear the soprano in the hands of a true jazz great. The soprano also features in lots of pop music—listen to Branford Marsalis on Sting's "Englishman In New York" for some really lovely soprano playing.

The difference between concert pitch and written pitch of the soprano is only one tone. The note C on a soprano sounds as a B♭ in concert pitch. The soprano is described as being in the key of B♭.

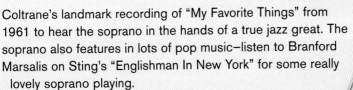

Curved soprano
Some soprano saxophones are curved in the same way as altos and tenors.

Non-curved soprano
More common than a curved soprano, the instrument is shaped like a clarinet and played away from the body.

SOPRANO SAXOPHONE RANGE (CONCERT PITCH)

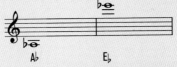

A♭   E♭

SOPRANO SAXOPHONE RANGE (WRITTEN PITCH)

B♭   F

Alto saxophone

The alto saxophone is possibly the most common and often the favorite for beginners because it's easier to play than the soprano and not as bulky and cumbersome as the tenor or baritone.

It is possible to play the alto sax in a huge range of styles, from the warm, lush sound of Johnny Hodges leading the Duke Ellington saxophone section to the fiery and groundbreaking Charlie Parker in the 1940s and '50s. More contemporary players have also made their own mark on the alto sax sound— Maceo Parker (with James Brown's band) and David Sanborn have given the alto saxophone a place in pop music.

The alto saxophone is also the most commonly used saxophone in classical music. Due to its late invention (the mid-nineteenth century) many of the great classical composers didn't write for the saxophone, however, the late romantic composers—Debussy in particular—contributed works to the saxophone repertoire.

The saxophone is also popular with contemporary composers: Takashi Yoshimatsu's "Fuzzy Bird Sonata" and Darius Milhaud's "Scaramouche" are popular works showcasing the alto saxophone.

Alto saxophone
The most popular with beginners, the alto saxophone is a manageable size and the favorite of many of the great players.

ALTO SAXOPHONE RANGE (CONCERT PITCH)

Db   Ab

ALTO SAXOPHONE RANGE (WRITTEN PITCH)

Bb   F

David Sanborn
Alto saxophone legend David Sanborn in action at the world-famous Montreux Jazz Festival.

Coleman Hawkins
The first great tenor saxophone player Coleman Hawkins (foreground) leading the way in the 1940s.

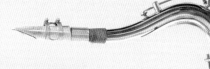

Tenor saxophone

Ever since Coleman Hawkins'
legendary recording of "Body and
Soul" in 1939, the tenor saxophone
has belonged to jazz. The deeper
range and variety of sounds and moods
available on the tenor saxophone
have enthralled generations of jazz
saxophonists from Hawkins and his
contemporary Lester Young, to John
Coltrane and Sonny Rollins in the 1950s
and '60s through to contemporary greats
Michael Brecker and Chris Potter.

Tenor saxophone
Bigger in size and
deeper in range than
the alto saxophone,
the tenor saxophone
is capable of a huge
range of dynamic and
tonal variety.

TENOR SAXOPHONE RANGE (CONCERT PITCH)

Ab   Eb

TENOR SAXOPHONE RANGE (WRITTEN PITCH)

Bb   F

Baritone saxophone

The baritone is the biggest of the four main saxophones and plays an octave below the alto. Most newer baritone saxophones have a low A and so go one note lower than the standard B♭ of the other saxophones. The low A is operated with the left thumb and is found below the thumb pad.

The baritone really comes into its own as a member of a saxophone section. The standard big band sax section consists of two altos, two tenors, and a baritone, and the low register of the baritone really can add weight to the section sound.

A notable baritone sax soloist is Gerry Mulligan. Mulligan made the cumbersome baritone sound light and elegant as a solo instrument—listen to Mulligan's quartet with trumpeter/vocalist Chet Baker in the 1960s. This is renowned as one of the great jazz small groups. The baritone also is a feature of the pop brass section—listen to Amy Winehouse's song "Rehab" and listen out for the baritone honking away at the bottom.

Baritone saxophone
One octave lower than the alto saxophone, the baritone is capable of a resonant, bassy sound.

BARITONE SAXOPHONE RANGE (CONCERT PITCH)

C   A♭

BARITONE SAXOPHONE RANGE (WRITTEN PITCH)

A   F

Gerry Mulligan
One of the preeminent
baritone saxophonists,
Mulligan produced a
light, elegant sound on
the baritone saxophone.

Saxophone manufacturers

There is an increasing number of saxophone makes and models on the market. Traditionally the French company Selmer have dominated the high end of the market with their classy saxophones. Yamaha and Yanagisawa make very high-quality instruments from entry-level to customized professional models. The German Keilwerth saxophones are also available in a range of prices and styles.

The British company Trevor James make very good affordable student models and are a good option for the beginner.

Breathing

All wind instruments require you to breathe at some point. While this can seem a hindrance at first it can actually be helpful to you as a musician as it makes you phrase your music—much like language, music can be thought of as smaller phrases (like sentences) grouped together to form a larger body. Having to breathe makes you subconsciously more aware of these phrases within a piece.

Saxophone music very rarely comes with all the breathing places marked for you—everyone is different and the choice of where to breathe is usually left up to the performer. As a beginner you will simply breathe when you want to or have run out of breath, but as you get more experienced you will develop a feel for when it's appropriate to breathe without interrupting the music and also for how long you can maintain a good sound with a lungful of air.

When learning a new piece, think about where the phrases start and end—try to imagine phrases like written language and breathe in the gaps created by the musical phrases. When you have decided where to breathe, mark the spot with a V sign in the gap between the notes—this is common practice and even top-level professional musicians do this.

Accessories

There are a number of accessories available for the saxophone—some are essential and others are optional extras you could consider as your playing improves.

Reeds

The reed is the only part of your saxophone that you will need to replace regularly. Reeds have a natural shelf life and will become soft and unresponsive over time. You will get a feel for when your reeds are past their best and need replacing, but aim to change the reed every few weeks—less if you aren't playing so much and more often if you are playing every day. You should always put the reed back in its holder when you've finished playing for the day. This will prolong the life of the reed and help to protect it too. Chipped reeds don't play so well!

Reeds are graded by strength and/or thickness—the thicker the reed the more rich and resonant the sound; however, thicker reeds are harder to play and require more control and

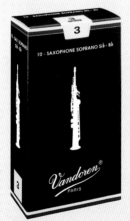

Soprano reeds
A box of reeds for the soprano saxophone—usually ten reeds per box.

Alto reeds
A box of reeds for the alto saxophone—usually ten reeds per box.

Tenor reeds
A box of reeds for the tenor saxophone—usually five reeds per box.

Baritone reeds
A box of reeds for the baritone saxophone—usually five reeds per box.

diaphragm strength. For less experienced players a softer reed is better to help build a good basic tone—you can then move up to thicker reeds.

Reeds start at strength No. 1 and move up in half steps to No. 5. It's a good idea to start at 1 or 1½ and move up as you feel ready. Note that some manufacturers grade the strength as "soft," "medium," or "hard" instead of numerical grades.

The choice of reeds is ever growing and there is an amount of trial and error involved in finding your favorite brand. Rico and Vandoren are the most popular, and La Voz and Hemke are also widely available.

Plastic/synthetic reeds

Plastic and synthetic reeds are a common alternative to traditional cane reeds. The life span is considerably longer and the reeds are more durable than the fragile cane reeds. Two popular manufacturers are Bari and Fibracell. Plastic reeds divide opinion—some people find them an easy and practical solution whereas other saxophonists find them difficult to play. As with your choice of brand and strength, it's really up to you.

Reed
Keep your reeds clean and replace when chipped for optimum sound quality.

Reed case
These come in different finishes from plastic to silver and can hold various numbers of reeds.

This way up
Remember always to put the thin end of the reed at the top of the mouthpiece.

Reed holder
Most reeds come in a plastic case, which keeps the reed flat and safe when you aren't playing.

Foil-wrapped reed
Foil wrapping will keep the reed fresh and moisture free.

Mouthpieces

Mouthpieces come in a variety of materials and sizes and can dramatically change the type of sound you produce. The standard mouthpiece supplied with your saxophone will be sufficient for some time, but if you want to upgrade your sound, a change of mouthpiece is the only solution.

The most common material for mouthpieces is Ebonite—a type of plastic. This is the choice for classical players and jazz players who wish for a light, mellow sound. Metal mouthpieces deliver a brighter, more edgy sound and are more suitable for pop and rock styles and a heavier, more robust jazz sound. There are many variables in saxophone mouthpieces—the size of the chamber, and the tip opening (the gap between the reed tip and the mouthpiece) all vary and change the sound and playability of the instrument.

As with reeds, trial and error is the only option if you are seriously looking for a new mouthpiece.

Ebonite mouthpiece
The V16 Vandoren range is aimed at jazz players who want a rich, dark tone.

Ebonite mouthpiece
Suitable for all musical styles and will play easily in both classical and jazz.

Metal mouthpiece
This style will produce a bright sound and project a loud and clear sound.

Gold-lacquered metal
This style is popular with jazz players wanting a robust, husky sound.

Other accessories

Other than your sax, mouthpiece, and reeds there isn't much else you need initially. There are optional accessories available that you may consider buying at a later date.

Saxophone sling
Comfort is all-important when you are playing your saxophone. Choose a sling that is comfortable against your neck and doesn't dig in.

Saxophone stand
A stand is useful as it means you can leave your instrument out between practice sessions. Saxophones look good as ornaments too!

Tuning

Tuning your saxophone is important for playing along with other musicians or backing tracks—a sharp (too high) or flat (too low) instrument can sound pretty bad. Traditionally musicians tune to an A (bear in mind that due to the transposition this is an F♯ for alto sax and a B for tenor sax). Play into the tuner and make sure your note is in tune. To make the note sharper push the mouthpiece farther onto the crook—to make the note flatter pull the mouthpiece farther off the crook.

Intonation

Intonation is similar to tuning but deals with the tuning relative to the instrument. Assume you have tuned your concert A but some of the high notes still sound out of tune— this means your intonation is off and you will need to correct the tuning of these notes yourself with a combination of your embouchure and breath control. This is an ongoing problem for all wind players— using a tuner can really help your intonation.

Tuner

A tuner is a helpful practice accessory because it allows you to check your tuning and correct your intonation.

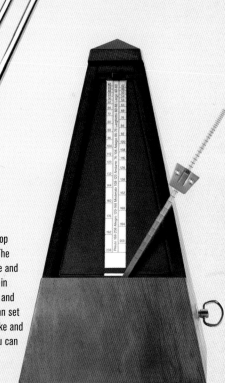

Metronome

A metronome will help you to develop the rhythmic side of your playing. The metronome will keep a steady pulse and enable you to play pieces or scales in strict time rather than speeding up and slowing down unnecessarily. You can set the metronome to any tempo you like and by gradually speeding up pieces you can easily measure your progress.

Cases

Your saxophone will come in a standard hard case—if you aren't carrying the instrument far this will protect it very well. However, solid cases are bulky and heavy to transport if you are walking and using public transportation. You can buy a variety of lightweight cases—often these are smaller and shaped to fit the saxophone more snugly and, crucially, have backpack-style shoulder straps to make transport easier. Cases are getting lighter all the time and the quality of protection is getting better too—good manufacturers included Bam, Hiscox, and Pro-Tec.

Ligatures

The ligature is the brace that holds the reed to the mouthpiece. In the early days of saxophone (and indeed clarinet) playing, the musician would simply tie the reed to the mouthpiece with a piece of cord or string. Technology has advanced since then, and different ligature manufacturers claim that their ligatures can enhance and vary the sound of the saxophone in many different ways. As you progress and become more aware of the sound you wish to make, you should experiment with different ligatures (any good saxophone store will let you try different accessories) and see which suits your sound and style best.

Leather ligature
Some ligatures are made of leather or fabric with a single screw at the top.

Ligature and cap
The ligature usually comes with a cap to cover the reed and mouthpiece when not in use.

Charlie Parker
Possibly the greatest alto saxophonist of them all, Charlie "Bird" Parker in full flight.

Caring for your saxophone

The day-to-day care of your saxophone shouldn't take too much time but regular cleaning is important. Each time you put your saxophone away you should make sure that you clean the reed and mouthpiece, wipe away any excess saliva, and make sure that the reed is dry before you put it into its cover.

Cleaning your saxophone

To clean the main body of the instrument you should use a "pull through." This is essentially a small cloth on a weighted piece of string that you drop down the saxophone and then pull through from the other end. This will clear any unwanted saliva and general moisture from the inside of your saxophone— if you leave all the moisture, it collects on the pads underneath the keys and can cause them to stick rather than opening and closing smoothly.

You should give your mouthpiece a good wash in the sink once in a while too; as it spends a lot of time in your mouth it can collect germs and prolong any illnesses you may have.

Cork grease
Apply grease to the cork section of the crook to allow you to move the mouthpiece smoothly on and off the crook.

Pull through
A simple cleaning device that allows you to clean through the inside of the saxophone and absorb excess moisture.

Branford Marsalis
Contemporary saxophone
great Branford Marsalis
in full swing on the
tenor saxophone.

Give your sax an annual service

Your saxophone should also go to a professional repairer for a service—how often depends on how much you play it and how often you feel it needs attention, but once a year is a good guideline. A repairer will check over the instrument for leaks and worn pads and generally ensure that the mechanism is still performing as it should. Often when you get your saxophone back from the repairer it feels like a dramatically improved instrument.

Practice

The golden rule with practice is a little and often—trying to cram two weeks' worth of work into one session the night before your lesson or gig isn't the most effective way to improve. The amount of time you can dedicate to your practice obviously depends on your work or school schedule, but try to play at least three times a week. Even if each session is short (10 to 15 minutes), this will benefit you more than a marathon session less often. Below is a rough guide to splitting your practice time effectively.

25% Long notes and scales	50% Pieces and exercises	25% Creative/fun work
This is the warm-up section of your practice and will get you warm and loose and ready to concentrate on making music. This is the equivalent of an athlete doing stretches before more vigorous exercise.	Pick a specific lesson or piece that you have been working on. Focus on playing the piece as accurately and musically as possible. Isolate any tricky passages and repeat these so that they become less problematic. Simply playing the piece from start to finish will only mean you are practicing the mistakes and uncertainties as part of the piece. Ask yourself how you are playing the piece—are you capturing the mood and style effectively?	Play music that you enjoy playing. This might be pieces you've previously learned and enjoyed, or you could work on some of the different styles approached in this book— you might want to play a twelve-bar blues and work on your improvising. This part of your practice should be the part when you really enjoy your music making—this, presumably, is why you started playing!

Away from the saxophone

You can also improve your musicianship away from the instrument. Music is all around us and you can grow as a musician just by listening. Many musicians and performances have been mentioned throughout this book—you could look them up on the Internet. Hearing the saxophone played really well is a great way to inspire yourself and focus on what you like and how you want to play.

John Coltrane
Tenor saxophonist John Coltrane pushed the emotional and technical boundaries of the instrument in ways no one had thought possible a generation earlier.

Joining a band

Having invested a lot of time in your practice and learned your skills on the instrument, it's now time to share your music with other people. Music is seldom a solitary pastime (except for personal practice) and there is very little music written for one instrument alone. Much of the fun of music making comes when you join an ensemble of some kind and start to add your voice to a group and meet other musicians.

Finding a band

Finding a group that suits you and is of the right standard can be difficult. Keep your eyes open—most music shops and rehearsal venues will have a notice board where musicians will put up flyers advertising for musicians. Talk to your teacher too—they may know the local scene well and be able to advise. If you have to audition, make sure that you are punctual and friendly—getting on with your colleagues is really important in music!

What kind of band?

There are many different sorts of groups and ensembles where the saxophone has a presence—on the following page is a brief guide to some of them.

Jazz band
Occidental Brothers Dance Band performs in Le Poisson Rouge as part of Winter Jazzfest in New York.

Orchestral music

Because it is such a young instrument (only used since the 1850s) the saxophone doesn't have a huge presence in orchestral music. There are works that require saxophone, but there is little call for a saxophone as a full-time member of an orchestra.

Wind band

An ensemble consisting of wind and brass instruments and percussion, a wind band plays a large variety of music from arrangements of orchestral music to theater songs and TV themes. Wind bands can be a great way to experience a variety of styles in a large group.

Big band

If you're interested in ensemble jazz playing, a big band is probably for you. The standard big-band saxophone section consists of two altos, two tenors, and a baritone, meaning that you can play alongside other saxophonists and compare notes. Big bands cover a wide range of repertoire from the classic sounds of the Count Basie and Duke Ellington orchestras through to the more contemporary Buddy Rich Band. Many of the tunes have sections for improvisation and you may well find chord symbols as well as written notes on your part.

Horn section

Since the brass section began to be used by Motown bands in the 1950s, it has been a feature of many pop, soul, and funk records. The size and instrumentation of the horn section varies but a popular combination is trumpet, saxophone, and trombone. Listen to Stevie Wonder's "Sir Duke" to hear really tight horn-section work.

Small jazz group

If you wish to focus more on improvisation, you may want to join or even start a smaller group like a quartet. The focus of small groups is improvisation and you will have a chance to stretch out in your solos.

Small jazz group
Joining a small jazz group will give you a chance to focus on your improvisation skills.

Symphony orchestra
Some contemporary classical pieces make use of the saxophone, but the vast majority of orchestral music was composed before the saxophone was invented.

5 Useful Information

This chapter will help you quickly check musical jargon. Throughout the book many terms and definitions have been introduced. The Glossary provides a list of all the terms and a quick explanation, and the Resources section provides a summary of musical notation. The Italian terms section covers some of the terminology used in written music—this is intended to help you interpret the music in terms of style, tempo, and mood.

Glossary

All the musical terms introduced in the book are explained on the following pages, providing a quick-reference guide.

Accidentals
The collective term for sharps and flats.

Arpeggio
The spelling out of a chord note by note on the saxophone. Major/minor arpeggios consist of the root note, third, and fifth of the scale.

Articulation
The use of the tongue to punctuate musical phrases. Good articulation or tonguing will give your playing a crisp, clear sound.

Bars
Music is divided into smaller units of time called bars. All bars have a set number of beats as denoted by the time signature.

Blue note
A note characteristic of the blues, often clashing with the tonality of the piece for effect.

Blues scale
A six-note scale characteristic of blues/soul/jazz music.

Call and response
A style of song featuring a repeated call with varying answering phrases.

Chord
A series of notes played together—impossible on the saxophone but common on the piano or guitar.

Chromatic scale
A scale consisting entirely of semitones. Because the gaps between the notes are all the same, all chromatic scales are identical, apart from the starting note.

Circle of fifths
A diagram showing the relationship between the 12 tones of the chromatic scale, and their major/minor keys and key signatures (see page 159). Moving clockwise around the circle from the top, the interval between each key is a perfect fifth.

Crook
The curved top section of the saxophone, which slots into the top of the main body of the instrument.

Dynamics
The collective term for the changes in volume within a piece.

Eighth-note
A note that is half a beat in length—sometimes called a quaver.

Embouchure
The position of your mouth when you are playing. A good embouchure is essential for a good tone.

Flat
A ♭ sign next to a note lowers it by a semitone.

Half-note
A two-beat note—sometimes called a minim.

Harmonic minor
A minor scale form. Has an Egyptian/Arabic sound.

Head
A term for the melody of a piece, mostly used by jazz musicians.

Improvisation
Spontaneous composition—making up melodies as you go along.

Interval
The distance between two notes, usually explained as a numerical distance—F to G is the interval of a second, F to A is a third etc.

Key
Most music is rooted in a key—this is a stable base for the music and to which everything else is related and contrasted. As with scales, major and minor keys are the norm.

Key signature
Each key has certain sharps and flats inbuilt to keep the shape and structure consistent with other keys. The key signature is written at the start of the piece and means certain notes are always sharp or flat throughout. A key signature should never mix sharps and flats.

Ledger lines
Extra horizontal lines added above and below the stave for times when the music goes higher or lower than the standard notes on the stave.

Ligature
The brace that holds the reed in place against the mouthpiece.

Major key
A bright/happy-sounding tonality.

Melodic minor
One of the minor scale variations, which differs in its ascending and descending forms.

Minor key
A sad/dark-sounding tonality.

Mouthpiece
The reed and mouthpiece are attached to the end of the saxophone and make up the part of the instrument you blow into. Mouthpieces are made of a variety of materials—plastic or ebonite are the most common but metal and sometimes wood are used too.

Octave
There are only 12 notes in Western music (C to B♭)—these can be repeated in higher and lower registers or "octaves."

Octave key
Operated by your left thumb, the octave key moves notes from one place in the lower register to the same place in the middle and upper registers.

Pentatonic scale
A five-note scale dating back hundreds of years. Pentatonic scales can be major or minor and are the backbone of a huge variety of musical styles.

Playing by ear
Playing melodies without written music straight from your head.

Quarter-note
A one-beat note—sometimes called a crotchet.

Reed
The piece of cane you attach to the mouthpiece to produce the sound. These come in different strengths (from 1–5) and will wear out over time, so always keep some spares in your case.

Relative major/minor
Every major key has a minor that shares its key signature. Count down three semitones to find the relative minor from a major key and up three semitones to find the relative major from a minor.

Rest
A period of silence in a piece. Rests come in the same lengths as notes: four beats, two beats, one beat etc.

Scale
A scale is a sequence of consecutive notes from a set starting point. Scales come in many different forms—major and minor being the most common.

Semitone
A half-step between two notes—F to F♯ is a semitone. This is the smallest interval in music.

Sharp
A ♯ symbol next to a note raises it by a half-step or semitone.

Side keys
The auxiliary keys on the saxophone are called side keys. These are often played with the inside of the hand rather than the ends of the fingers.

Sixteenth-note
A note that is a quarter beat in length—sometimes called a semiquaver.

Sling
A support for the saxophone that you put around your neck while playing. This helps support the instrument and takes some of the weight.

Slur
Notes joined together by a curved line are slurred. There should be no gap between the notes—they should move smoothly into each other.

Solo section
The part of a jazz piece dedicated to improvisation, usually a looped set of chords of a particular length repeated as many times as the improviser feels appropriate.

Stave
The set of five horizontal lines onto which music is written.

Swung eighth-notes
Used in jazz and swing music, swung eighth-notes make the first of each pair of eighth-notes longer than the second.

Syncopation
A style of playing that involves interesting off-beat rhythms, popular in jazz music.

Tie
Two notes of the same pitch joined together like a slur are "tied."

Time signature
The symbol by the clef at the start of the piece will tell you how many beats are in each bar and what sort of beats they are. 4/4 is the most common. Time signatures can also be a clue to the type of piece—a 3/4 piece is often a waltz.

Tone
The distance between two consecutive notes—the distance between F and G is a tone.

Treble clef
The ornate symbol at the far left of the stave, which shows the register that the music is in. All saxophone music is written in the treble clef, since it is consistent with the range of the instrument.

Triplet
Three notes in the space of two quarter-note triplets are a set of three notes in the space of two quarter-notes.

Twelve-bar blues
A twelve-bar song form immortalized by the blues but used in many different settings.

Verse and chorus
Many songs are structured around verses and choruses. The chorus is usually the same each time and is often the most memorable section. The verses often change slightly either in terms of melody or lyrics.

Whole-note
A four-beat note—sometimes called a semibreve.

Resources

Notation in a nutshell

TREBLE CLEF
All music for the saxophone is written in the treble clef.

TIMING
Tells you the time signature. Here, the symbol is 4/4. The upper number shows how many beats per bar and the lower number represents the note-value of the beat.

BAR LINE
Notation is organized into bars. Bar lines are the vertical lines that separate the bars.

FLAT
A flat sign indicates that the note must lower in pitch by a semitone. The symbol may appear at the beginning of a piece of music (known as a key signature) or next to a particular note (known as an accidental). An accidental continues for the rest of the bar unless a natural sign overrides it.

NATURAL
Indicates the note must be played normally, ignoring the key signature or a previous accidental in the measure.

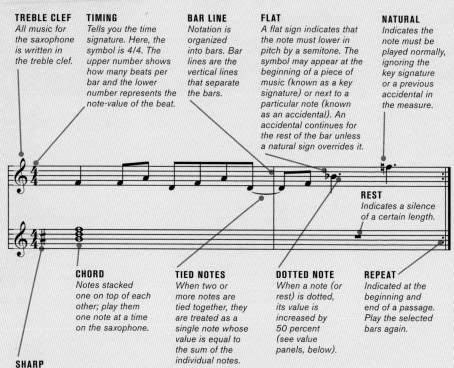

REST
Indicates a silence of a certain length.

CHORD
Notes stacked one on top of each other; play them one note at a time on the saxophone.

TIED NOTES
When two or more notes are tied together, they are treated as a single note whose value is equal to the sum of the individual notes.

DOTTED NOTE
When a note (or rest) is dotted, its value is increased by 50 percent (see value panels, below).

REPEAT
Indicated at the beginning and end of a passage. Play the selected bars again.

SHARP
A sharp sign indicates that the note has to be raised in pitch by a semitone. The symbol may appear at the beginning of a piece of music (known as a key signature) or next to a particular note (known as an accidental). An accidental continues for the rest of the bar unless a natural sign overrides it.

For more about note and rest values see Lessons 3 and 5.

Note	Value
𝅝	4 beats
𝅗𝅥	2 beats
♩	1 beat
♪	½ beat
𝅘𝅥𝅯	¼ beat
𝅘𝅥𝅰	⅛ beat

Rest	Value
▬	4 beats
▬	2 beats
𝄽	1 beat
𝄾	½ beat
𝄿	¼ beat
𝅀	⅛ beat

Summary of note names

Below is a summary of the range of notes on the saxophone, shown on the stave and labeled for easy reference. When you are learning to read music, it will be useful to study the diagram to help cement the notes in your head.

Web sites and music books

- www.saxontheweb.net
- www.reeds-direct.co.uk
- www.sax.co.uk
- www.youtube.com
A great resource for watching musicians at work.
- *Charlie Parker Omnibook*—Charlie Parker's solos transcribed accurately from the records. An essential resource for bebop aficionados.
- *The New Real Book*—a must for jazz musicians, the real book contains hundreds of essential tunes.
- *15 Easy Jazz Etudes*, Bob Mintzer—well written and fun pieces with CD backing.
- *Sonata G Minor BWV 1020*, J. S. Bach—originally for violin and piano, this sonata works very well on saxophone.
- *20 Modern Studies For Solo Saxophone*, James Rae—interesting modern pieces by a leading figure in wind education.
- *Artist Transcriptions: John Coltrane*—original Coltrane solos.
- *Artist Transcriptions: Julian "Cannonball" Adderley*—original Cannonball solos.
- *Stan Getz: Bossa Novas For Tenor Saxophone*—Stan Getz's beautiful Latin jazz playing transcribed for tenor saxophone.
- *Guest Spot: Jazz Solos Playalong For Alto Saxophone*—jazz solos with CD backing.
- *Easy Gershwin For Alto Saxophone*—some of Gershwin's best-loved tunes arranged for alto saxophone and piano.
- *Exploring Jazz Saxophone*, Ollie Weston—an introduction to jazz and improvisation.

Italian terms

Classical musical notation has always been in Italian—here is a list of some common Italian terms and their meanings in English.

Tempo

The pace of a piece of music is called the tempo. The terms are nonspecific and require some interpretation. Some more modern music will have an exact BPM (beats per minute) instruction and allows the player to set the tempo precisely using a metronome (see page 227).

Largo	Slow and stately.	*Presto*	Fast.
Lento	Slowly, but not as slow as largo.	*Accelerando*	Speeding up.
Adagio	Slowly, but not as slow as lento.	*Ritardando* (**Rit.**)	Slowing down.
Andante	At a walking pace.	*Rallantando*	A gradual slowing down.
Moderato	At a moderate tempo.		
Allegro	Lively.	*Rubato*	Freely, not in strict time.

Extra terms

The following terms can be added to other instructions to give a little more information.

Molto	Very.
Molto rubato	Very freely.
Poco	Little.
Poco crescendo	Increase in volume a little.
Ma non troppo	But not too much.
Largo ma non troppo	Slowly but not too slowly.

Dynamics

pp Pianissimo	Very quiet.
p Piano	Quiet.
mp Mezzo piano	Medium quiet.
mf Mezzo forte	Medium loud.
f Forte	Loud.
ff Fortissimo	Very loud.
Crescendo	Becoming louder.
Decrescendo	Becoming quieter.

Mood/expression

These words give you some clue as to the mood of the piece and should help you to get into the style.

Affettuoso	With feeling/affection.	*Con moto*	With movement.
Agitato	Agitated.	*Dolce*	Sweetly.
Animato	Animated.	*Grazioso*	Gracefully.
Cantabile	In a singing style.	*Maestoso*	Majestically.
Con amore	With love.	*Misterioso*	Mysteriously.
Con fuoco	With fire.	*Vivace*	Vivaciously/lively.
Con brio	With spirit/energy.		

Accents

Staccato	A staccato or dot over a note means it should be short and tongued.
Tenuto	A tenuto or dash symbol over a note means it should be smooth and sustained.
Long accent	A > over a note means it should be short and accented.
Short accent	A ^ over a note means it should be accented at the beginning and played for its full length.
Pause	A pause mark over a note means hold this note for longer—the duration is up to you or the person directing the piece, but essentially the pulse of the piece stops, then restarts in time if necessary. Pauses are often marked at the end of a piece and you should hold the last note for as long as you feel is appropriate.

Index

Acknowledgments

Quarto would like to thank the following agencies for supplying images for inclusion in this book:

p.40, 47, 55, 61, 69, 76, 81, 94, 99, 120, 133, 134, Rex Features; p.91, 117, Getty; p.13 Corbis

All step-by-step and other images are the copyright of Quarto Publishing plc. While every effort has been made to credit contributors, Quarto would like to apologize should there have been any omissions or errors—and would be pleased to make the appropriate correction for future editions of the book.